UNSCARRED

Falling Forward and Finding Strength in Life's Challenges

Angela D. Holmes

This book is dedicated to the Father, Son, and Holy Spirit. My life is hidden in you, your unwavering hand brought me through, sustained me, healed me and strengthened me. Isaiah 43 was your promise to me in the midst of the storm. I breathe because you live in me.

~Your Daughter, Angela

Beauty in the Midst of Chaos

CONTENTS

ACKNOWLEDGMENTS

I dedicate this book to the trailblazers, the resilient women that have endured the trauma of divorce and lived to tell how they grew through it. To the many strong men and women that God purposely placed in my life to impact and provoke me to shift into purpose.

Mommy:

To my mother Lenora Richardson, my heroine, my champion. I watched your strength, your resilience, and your poise in the most difficult situations. Because of you, I am the mother that I am today. You're my She'roe. God blessed me with the best mother on this side of Heaven. I'm strong today because of you, and I love you to pieces, Mommy.

My Why:

To my children, my WHY (Princess Ali, Prince Junie, and Mr. Myles) my rocks, my troopers. You make being a mommy easy. Because of you, my breath makes a difference in life. Thank you for letting mommy steal away. The days and nights of "not right now" all had a purpose. I would give my last breath for you. My prayer for you is that you keep God first and find the courage to impact this world, live fulfilled, and do what you love the most. I encourage you to live on purpose, follow the path God has destined for you, and always surround yourself with people who force you to do better. Remember that your words, behaviors, habits, and values become your destiny! God blessed me with you on purpose. As mommy always says, "Do your best, be your best!"

Shepherds and TIP-ites:

To my dearest Shepherds, Quentin and Tamara Bennett, words cannot express the honor that I have for you. God placed me in your hearts on purpose. Thank you for your unfailing love and support, all the unspoken pushes in the spirit. When I wanted just to warm the pew you made it too hot for me to sit in it by handing me the mic to pray and intercede. You saw in me what I did not see in myself. To the most supportive spiritual family I know, "We are stronger together." TIP (This Is Pentecost) Fellowship Ministries, Sacramento/Oakland, God purposely placed us in each other's hearts, a family with a driven passion for the heart of God and deliverance of souls, I love you!

My Siblings and Loves:

Connie, Victor, Craig and Banbury, I love you to pieces. We are characters in our own right. LOL! Helen

Jenkins and Trena Watson, your true friendship that began in the infancy of our lives has impacted my life more than you know. Monica, Celestine, Diamond, and Crystal, your support and tears will never be forgotten. Vivian Goodbeer and Georgia Robinson thank you for your selfless commitment to this project. It would never have come to be without your obedience to the Lord. Your friendship is precious and unforgettable.

Asha Tyson, my mentor and business coach, such a Godsend. You exemplify a true *Diamond!* You have poured out your gifting and knowledge so unselfishly. Thank you for seeing what God has ordained for me. Thank you for obeying your call. I truly thank God for you!

Cannon Publishing thank you for molding my project. To the many loving, selfless, giving, imparting, uplifting, and encouraging vessels, I've met along this journey, oh, how I applaud you for allowing God to use you to impact my life. Manifold blessings to you.

PROLOGUE

How bad do you want it? How determined are you to win?
~Dr. Tamara Bennett

When I stopped making excuse after excuse, I began to see how I can make life work well. Pain is inevitable in life, and so is purpose. You can't have one without the other. Learning this has allowed me to free myself from self-destructive thoughts and habits. We all have a very meaningful purpose in life. We were purposely created before time began. We were intentionally pre-destined with purpose. We were specifically created, and were unique, and planted deep inside of each of us is absolutely everything we need to fulfill the purpose God created us for.

Life Lesson: It really doesn't matter where you are right now in your life. No matter whether you are successful or have failed miserably, God is still growing you and birthing your dreams. Destiny lies within you. God won't give up, so you shouldn't either. Forget what hurt you in the past, but never ever forget what it taught you! I know that you have often experienced the very hard task of relating your pain to a God-given purpose. It's easy for your purpose to get lost in the pain if you don't search for the hidden pearl it represents. Do you find yourself masking your toughest battles? Trying to hide away the days of emotional pain, the hours of intense confusion, the moments of anger, and the seconds of the daunting "why?" Have you ever taken the time to process the circumstances that caused the pain? Most have not, including me. You're not alone.

You need to have the right image on the inside. How you see yourself either impose limits or determines your level of success and how far you will go in life. We can fall victim to our place of chaotic comfort, not realizing that we are the absolute sum product of our very thoughts. When I learned this principle, it changed my outlook on pain. I realized that I have the power in my thoughts to change my life.

Psalms 23:7 is a powerful thought to meditate on: "As a man thinketh in his heart, so is he." Something so ordinary can change your life to extraordinary. Purpose is intentional. It is a carefully etched plan with rewards.

Pain is a power packed agitate that precedes purpose. I ran from pain for most of my life, never wanting to experience heartache, mental stress, or combative situations. When faced with these seeming enemies of society, my way to resolve them was to tuck them away and bury them; never dealing with them. This choice placed me in very uncomfortable positions later in life.

Life's challenges are an indication of where you will best succeed. The lessons I learned on my journey of dealing and healing were so explosive that I was instructed to share my struggle and my pain. In 2012, a study initiated by Mary Kay, Inc. found that "74% of survivors stayed with an abusive partner for longer than they wanted to because of financial concerns." Most women fear financial struggle and loneliness. Ending an abusive relationship is not easy for most, and recovering and thriving in life afterward is not often the case. A study by the National Institute for Healthcare Research in Rockville, MD reports that divorced men and women are three times as likely to commit suicide, stemming from the lost hope of recovering. This is alarming! Life is not over—we have to know that we can get up dust ourselves off. Your marriage ended, not your life.

Imagine what you can do to impact the world when you heal and find purpose. Are you willing to heal? If you aren't willing to go through the process necessary to heal, then you're not yet ready. The only way to recover is through healing, and admitting you need to do it is the first step. God will put you in situations to help you work out what you asked God to take out.

Are you willing to be selfless and determined to impact someone else's life story? In the end, let your most devastating pain mold and create your greatest strength.

Now, let's take a walk through my journey of healing. Developing the courage to write in such transparency was life-altering. While I began to pen my journey and take healing steps, I was smack dab in the midst of my molding process. As I have done so often in the past, I began discounting my ability—as if I could have done it all under the power of my own strength—but *God* orchestrated it all, not me. Lives are waiting to be changed through power-packed testimonies. You have one too— make it known!

When you can't see in the dark, remember what God said
in the light. ~Unknown

Throughout this book, I will pour out what God poured into me—my choice to fight based on promise, purpose, prize and my determination to achieve irrevocable emotional healing. God gave me the title *Unscarred* to let you know that only God can heal a wound and remove the scar. "For I will close up thy scar, and will heal thee of thy wounds, saith the Lord. Because they have called thee, this is Zion, an outcast: This is she that hath none to seek after her" (Jeremiah 30:17).

Surrender to the process, go through the steps and allow God to purge and purify you so that you can find and fulfill your purpose in life. Blessings, peace, and great grace to you.

Because He has my heart, I can live Unscarred!
~ Angela D. Holmes

PART ONE |

EXTERNAL COMPONENTS

CHAPTER ONE: **THE ROOT**

If you don't know how the enemy got in, you don't know how to shut the door. It has to be dealt with and cut at the root! ~Dr. Tamara Bennett

Root *noun* [\ˈrüt, ˈru̇ t\]: *the part of a plant that grows underground, gets water from the ground, and holds the plant in place;* something that is an **origin or source**; *the essential core; close relationship with an environment. (Merriam-Webster)*

The word ***root*** is often used throughout the Bible. It depicts something grounded, something set firmly and securely, not shallow but deeply embedded to produce growth for good—or for evil. The enemy understands this concept and knows that he needs to plant his seeds deep down in our souls as early as possible in our lives. He knows they have to take root and hold strong to be effective and produce their like kind.

When our character, our emotions, and our daily feelings don't match the promises of God, we should diligently seek the root of that which is affecting us and keeping us from the true grace that the Lord has given us— the grace to live a life with joy, peace, and great expectations of inevitable good things in every situation.

My life was engulfed with roots of dysfunction, and my lack of knowledge about how to fight through prayer caused me great grief and despair.

Digging Deep

Each year, an estimated minimum of 3. 3 million children witness domestic violence.

While struggling through the wilderness of finding my true purpose, my course was strategically designed to rid my soul of all heaviness. I asked the Lord to show me the root of the dysfunction that had plagued me since I was a child. When I asked God to show me where the rejection, oppression, violence, anger, lack of confidence, distrust of people, shyness, passiveness, unforgiveness, suicidal thoughts, regression, bitterness, lack of self-esteem and self-worth had come from, He began to unveil my childhood to me in the days to come. It was time for me to be healed and set free. The path I would need to take to do this was not my choice, but my obedience to God's direction released me.

Daly City, California

Dissociated trauma memories don't reveal themselves like ordinary memories. Like pieces of a puzzle, they escape the primitive part of our brain where the trauma has been stored without words. ~Jeanne McElvaney

Before I realized that my childhood was dysfunctional, nightmares, post-traumatic stress disorder, and emotional struggles were not abnormal to me. The roots of my dysfunctional thinking and damaged emotions were generated in my childhood. As I began to have vivid dreams that would take me back to my childhood, I remembered detailed décor and specific days, times, and events. I always had a guide in my dreams, and this guide would take me back to my home in Daly City, California. In most of my dreams, I pleaded to leave. My guide pointed things out to me, but would not let me go.

There was one dream more notable than the rest. It revealed a rape in my home, in my former bedroom, but I could not see the rapist. In the dream, I didn't want to face it. I just wanted to leave and pleaded desperately to go. The emotion that came with the dream was too much to bear, and

I woke up in a panic. Night after night, my dreams would land me in the home I grew up in on Whittier Street—the root of my dysfunction.

Rejection, physical and verbal abuse took root early in my life. I'm the youngest of five children—. It was 1973, and we moved from San Francisco's Hunters Point area to Daly City, California when I was four years old. Daly City was a small family-oriented city at that time, and racism was prevalent. African Americans were discouraged from purchasing homes in this suburban area, but my parents pursued and won. I knew nothing of the dynamics of the move—I was just happy to have a new room, a garage with a huge playroom, and backyard to play in.

My childhood was not all bad. There were good days of laughter, playing Hot Wheels with my brothers, tag with neighbors, and watching lots of *The Three Stooges*, *Underdog*, and my favorite, *Scooby Doo*. I have good memories of going to the War Memorial Center for dances with the DJ Big Bob as I got older, memories of songs like "I'm Ready" by Kano, "Radio" by LL Cool J, and songs by Soul Sonic Force and Afrika Bambaataa. I remember having a crush on Marko Mesa and hanging with the Cholos and Cholas (A group of Latin individuals, male and female) on

Mission and Templeton Street, a popular local bus transfer location. The good ole '80s was a classic time in history.

In the early '70s, all of my siblings lived in our home. Little by little, this began to change. I have early memories of my Daddy being kind and talking to me, often preferring me over the other children. I climbed on him, sat in his lap, and took rides with him everywhere he went. I sat on the middle armrest in his white on white 1968 Cadillac Fleetwood Brougham, happy and content.

This would change drastically—or maybe it had always been there but wasn't evident.

The Abuse

This seemingly happy family was, in fact, a tumultuous physically and mentally abusive home. My Daddy was known to others as Roscoe, Fuller, or Robert… he had many names. Roscoe could be cruel, violent, and manipulative. He was a mentally ill man. He was older, and uneducated and was embarrassed by his illiteracy, which caused a great deal of his agitation. He grew up on a poor farm in Houston, Texas, quite possibly in the '20s and '30s. We never really knew his age and, in doing my research on Roscoe, his death certificate does not show a birth date, but he was much older than my mother—at least twenty-five years her senior; if I'm not mistaken. He spent his life as a young adult in the impoverished areas of Houston's Wards, which was according to his account of childhood and adulthood memories. He was an abuser, so I assumed he most likely endured abuse by his family. (This was my way of trying to make sense of it all). At that time in the Southwest, racism most definitely contributed to his torment and anguish. Unfortunately, the entire family was held hostage by his emotional issues.

An abuser will blame others for all problems or for the abuser's own shortcomings.

My first memory of abuse was when I was about five or six years old. All the kids were living in the home at this particular time. I vividly remember playing with my Baby That-A-Way when the fighting began. When it was over, Roscoe told me, "Look what you did! You made me do this to her—this is your fault." He had my mother by the arm, and she stood there with tears in her eyes, her face and neck bruised, and said nothing. As the years went on so did the abuse.

So traumatic were these incidents that it still feels as if it just happened yesterday. I can recount each incident and see them all clearly, and they tormented me for years to come. The feeling that every fight was my fault and hearing Roscoe say how my mother loved her children more than him and then abusing her for it didn't help either. He would get jealous if it seemed to him like we showed more attention to her than we did to him. He pumped so much fear into my siblings and me, and it worked—we feared Roscoe. From the time of this incident, I truly believed that every one of her beatings was my fault. Of course, that wasn't the truth, but when abuse is embedded in you at such an early age, it becomes you, and you become it. He found multiple reasons to argue with my mother based on what we the children did. If we were too loud or if he thought she showed us too much attention, he would argue and hit her. I couldn't hug her or be close to her in his presence. Whenever he left the house, I clung to her and would run to my room when I heard the garage door open, which meant he was back. I adapted and learned when to hug and cuddle with my mommy—and when not to. I lived in anxiety, not knowing when the next violent outbreak would occur but always alert to the clear and present danger.

Abuse Becomes Embedded

It is ironic how with abuse if it's not dealt with or destroyed, it seems to compound and get worse. Watching your mother being choked and slapped and hearing the sounds of flesh on flesh and her pleas for him to stop was an unrelenting and tormenting bell that rang and rang and never stopped.

The abuser may expect children to perform beyond their capability.

It was as if Roscoe had an addiction to abuse. Whenever we did something wrong, this physical abuse would turn on us. It brought an extension cord whipping which left welts and pain that never seemed to go away. I cried every time someone got a whipping. I became fearful and was afraid to say, do, or touch anything. I learned never to be wrong, to not ask questions, and to not talk back. Everything scared me, but as a child, you don't see these signs—you just try to make sense of life—therefore, fear became normal.

Children who grow up with abuse are expected to keep the family secret.

It was an unspoken understanding that you never tell what went on in our home. Roscoe ran a tight ship. He began a campaign of control and fear early on. He didn't allow us to look him in the eye—he felt as if we were challenging him when we did. So, I learned not to look at Roscoe—or anyone else—in the eye from that point on.

As I continue to think back on what seemed to be happier times, I remember when my parents decided to start a limousine business in 1977 when I was in the fourth grade. At that time, we were the only African-American limousine owners in Daly City and San Francisco. This business decision temporarily changed the atmosphere in the home.

An abusive person assumes the worse and is easily insulted.

Healing Key – Healing takes you through a process of collecting the broken pieces. Oftentimes, there are no words for what we feel. These small steps take a surmountable amount of heroic courage to face. Constant emotional and physical abuse becomes deeply embedded in you. It will take your personal truth to overcome the enemy's words which have been impressed upon you from childhood or in a long-term abusive relationship. God is the source of our strength, hope, and healing. Your determination to heal should not be based on your feelings, but instead based on His promises.

Isolation

An abuser will attempt to isolate the victim by severing the victim's ties to outside support and resources.

One way Roscoe controlled us was by isolation. We were not allowed to have anyone in the house without his permission. I could have two neighborhood friends visit from time to time and sometimes we could have friends play in the garage, but they had to be quiet. When we were all in the home, it was a ticking time bomb. You didn't know who was going to do or say something wrong that would release his fury. When my mother could have visitors, he would find something to fight with her about as soon as they left. He'd accuse her of not showing him enough attention and use that as an excuse to abuse my mother. Early on, my grandmother, Big Mama, and my Great-Aunt Mattie would visit, but that was soon disallowed. No one could come into the home— not our friends, not our family, and not our neighbors.

Children who are exposed to battering become fearful and anxious.

Hearing the sounds of my mother being beaten through my bedroom door was tearing me apart. It was as if I could feel every blow to my mother's face. I heard his fist smacking her flesh, her gagging as he choked her, and her cries of pain. Listening to this horror was torture. I squinted and blinked with every blow and would hide in my closet, crying and trembling. I began learning how to close my ears and count until it was over.

Children who grow up with abuse are expected to keep the family secret, sometimes not even talking to each other about the abuse.

Even when my brothers and sister were there, we all knew to go to our rooms and keep quiet. We didn't talk about it. I was helpless, paralyzed with fear, and I could do nothing to stop it. I would look at my mother and hug her when I could. She never frowned, and she never talked about it. My mother's love for me was always evident. She had a skillful way of loving me, she remained poise, even tempered and kind. She exemplified remarkable skill and emotional mastery in my presence. Her choice to do this in the midst of chaos was an extraordinary way of protecting me. She was a phenomenal mother, I adored her and often thought that I could not live life without her. I wanted to protect her, but I could not.

Rejection

Children of abuse feel isolated and vulnerable. They are starved for attention, affection, and approval.

The first real memory I have of rejection is when I was about five years old. I was invited to a neighbor's home for her birthday party, and my sister took me to the party. What I didn't know was that this day would remain as a focal point of rejection for me; even more, it would become a catalyst. Although I was invited to the party, I was apparently invited just to be taunted. (I really think the girl didn't invite me. I think her mother did.) During the party, I was pushed away by the other girls and blatantly not included. I remember sitting alone on the sofa with nothing to do. I told the little girl's mother, but she did nothing to make me feel included. I watched them play and laugh at me, ridiculing me, but I couldn't leave because my sister wouldn't take me home. I told her what was happening and was more disheartened when she replied that no one liked me and that's why I didn't have any friends.

The rejection by childhood friends planted a deeply set seed. I was quite traumatized and don't believe I ever recovered because I longed for acceptance and happiness for many years after this event. I continued to grow up with these same children. They disliked me and bullied me daily up until middle school. These mean girls would taunt and torment me about my hair and how fat I was. They'd taunt me with the typical "you think you're so cute" remarks. Oh, how I hate the jealousy—it grips girls so early in life. I was even teased based on what my parents owned, their cars, and their business—things that were my parents', not mine. I owned nothing because I was just a kid. I had a sister I admired and looked up to, but we never had the relationship I desired because she was very mean to me. My relationship with her was short-lived. She would repeatedly tell me she hated me, and I remember the crushing effect this had on my heart. These things may seem minuscule, but they are enormous when you're a child and marked by God. The enemy will magnify and release everything just to destroy God's creations—by any means necessary.

As a young girl, I occupied my time with dolls, and I had lots of them. My favorite doll was Dancerina. I had many stuffed animals and an imaginary friend named Maynard. I talked to them and made them my family. My imaginary time with my dolls was always happy. They loved me, and I loved them. Pretending that they were my family was how I escaped the pain of my real family's situation.

Back home, I continued to long for the attention of my sister, but it never happened. My relationship with my sister was the second key point from which the depths of rejection would manifest. Unfortunately, I don't have many happy memories of her. I remember the verbal and physical abuse. We shared a room and a bed, so when I got too close to her side, she would kick me hard and repeatedly until I moved. She would tell me she hated me, and I never knew why. I would cry and often wonder why.

I also remember that she never wanted to take me with her when my mother sent her places. To be honest, I was a very active child and had a short attention span, which may have played a part. In this day and time, I would have been labeled as overly hyperactive, but I saw myself as being interested in a lot of things all at once (smile). I was also very clingy and always wanted to be embraced.

One day, before we had a washer and dryer in the home, my sister and I went out to wash the clothes. We were getting ready to cross a busy street, and I ran into the street. She had to run and grab me, and we both almost got hit by a car. She slapped me so hard that I felt as if my neck would never straighten up again! I cried out loudly in pain and fear. I wanted so badly for her to love me because I wanted to be like her. I wanted to wear her clothes and her fancy platforms—I thought she had it going on.

Abandonment

These children become physically, emotionally, and psychologically abandoned.

When I was about eight years old, and my sister and I were in San Francisco on Mission Street. I can't remember why we were there or what we were doing, but I do recall that a short while after we arrived on Mission Street, she called our mom from a pay phone booth asking her to pick us up (so I thought). Then she called someone else, but I didn't know what the second call was about. I remember this being one of the longest waits I ever had. As we waited, a small Toyota pulled up, and she got in. She told me to wait at the bus stop for our mom. I asked her where she was going and if I could go with her, and she said no. I looked into the car—there was a man driving and a woman in the passenger seat with very large round glasses looking through the window at me. I begged her not to leave me, but she did. My sister was running away to go and live with her dad, and I didn't have a clue. I thought, *"How can they leave me here?"* I was so scared. What was going on? Where was she going without me? I sat and began to cry as I waited all alone, not knowing how I was going to get home. I was scared this incident initiated my fear of being left alone

When my mom came, she called the police. I remember going to the Daly City Police Department. Because I was so young, they had me draw pictures of what I remembered. I drew the car that I saw and the lady in the front seat with the big round glasses. I'll never forget how she looked at me over her shoulder as they drove off.

At home, I overheard conversations and arguments between my parents. My sister had run away. I never knew the truth nor was I allowed to talk to her on the phone or to any of my mom's relatives. My Great-Aunt Mattie, who loved me so very much—the only love I could really feel at the time—couldn't come over anymore either, and that made me very sad. She was always happy, gave me great big kisses and held me close.

As time went on, I began to realize why my sister ran away, but I became bitter towards her for leaving me alone. Soon after she left, my big brother left, too. One day, he just never came home. I have a very vague memory of him. There are only pictures to tell the story of our relationship as brother and sister. As it turns out, my brother and sister have the same father, so my brother, also went to live with his father. *What in the world is going on? They have another father?* I pondered. I kept asking where my brother was, but I was never told the truth, and a huge surge of abandonment overtook me. Roscoe separated us from my mother's family, and we weren't allowed to accept phone calls or visits by our relatives for years. My siblings and relatives' pictures were cut out of our photo books. I began to see them as the enemy and no longer a part of our family. As time went on, seclusion, secrets, and isolation set in on our house. No one visited, and no one called. When the phone did ring, sometimes people would hang up, and every call was scrutinized.

The physical abuse on my mother progressed, and when I was about twelve, my mother found the strength to leave Roscoe and the abuse. (Sadly, this was only for a brief period). We fled to Oakland, California and moved in with my sister and her husband temporarily. Now twelve, I hadn't seen my sister and brother for years. When I finally did see them, I didn't really know them or how to connect with them. It was such a strange feeling. What the heck! I was confused—I had only a distant memory of them, and because in the time since they had left, I had heard only that they were the enemy and that they had lied on Roscoe; therefore, negative feelings began to surface.

Anger

Children of domestic abuse may also use violence to express themselves and may display increased aggression with peers.

When I enrolled at Westlake Elementary School in Oakland, California, I felt so free. Life would be different, I thought. I saw my grandmother and great-aunt again, but I kept my distance from my sister because I kept thinking about how she had treated me, and I really didn't know what to do or think. I couldn't relate to her—and I didn't want to. I gave up trying to figure everything out.

I quickly learned that I had a lot of bottled up anger. Not long after being at my new school, I got into a fight right in the classroom. This girl had the nerve to tell me that she was going to beat me up. Wrong time in my life to bother me, missy. See, I began to be very reserved and quiet when I was in a fearful situation—I didn't let people see my anger right away—but I would unleash it as needed. I told her, "No, you're not," and she pushed me. Why did she do that? I socked her with my fist and tried to knock her clean through the classroom wall. To her shame, I mopped the floor with her. I was kicking her and pounding her head in a rage while I was on her back. The teachers had to pull me off. I was breathing hard and crying at the same time. Well, she never bothered me again. I had broken a projector and turned over a few chairs in the process, and my mom wasn't happy about the bill she received to pay for those items. My anger had been set loose, and that was not good. I knew I needed to be careful with myself. I had snapped big time, and it wasn't the last time it happened.

Power and Control

Women return to abusive relationships because they lack finances, fear handling life alone, have nowhere to go,

*have low self-esteem, need love, or believe that abuse is
normal.*

*Children who grow up observing their mothers being
abused, especially by their fathers, grow up with a role
model of intimate relationships in which one person uses
intimidation and violence over the other person to get
their way.*

My mother had no money and had to find a job, but all she knew was the limousine business. After struggling financially for months—and for other reasons I do not know—my mother eventually went back to Roscoe. I remember her asking my middle brother (let's call him George) if he wanted to go with her or stay with his dad. I didn't know he had a different dad just like the other two, but I guess he chose his dad because he didn't come with us. His departure added to the feelings of abandonment I already harbored. George and I had played all the time. He was so nice to me, and I was heartbroken beyond description, and I began to wonder why did he leave me?

We returned to Daly City when I was in the seventh grade. I went back to Colma Middle School and reconnected with my best friend, Helen. Everyone was asking me where I had been and what had happened. I was so ashamed, so I lied and said my parents had moved to Oakland and then we moved back. Not soon after we returned, the beatings started again, and the tormenting sound of these beatings made my insides cringe. Roscoe's violent temper became more aggressive and abusive after we returned. I was now thirteen years old, and my fear was heightened almost to the point of being unbearable.

Side Fact: *In 1979, psychologist Lenore Walker found that many violent relationships follow a common pattern or cycle. The tension building phase is a period of time in which tension builds over common domestic issues like money, children, or jobs. Verbal abuse begins in this first phase, triggering fear. An acute battering episode occurs when the tension peaks and the physical violence is on the rise and begins. It is usually triggered by the presence of an external event or by the abuser's own emotional state. Then the honeymoon phase. The abuser is ashamed of his/her behavior and expresses a surface remorse. He/she may then show loving, kind behavior followed by apologies, generosity, and helpfulness.*

As a young girl, I learned to hide and carry on as if all was normal. There would be times when I would not come out of my room even to use the bathroom. I would hold it or use my garbage can. I always felt I was going to be beaten next. So, I would wait until Roscoe went to bed, then I would clean my can and get something to eat—quietly. Most of the time, I would listen by the door first to see if he was snoring before I did anything. I learned his ways, his daily patterns, and maneuvered my life in the home around Roscoe. I knew that when he went to the bathroom in the middle of the night, it was usually about 2:00 am. I was on alert and listened attentively. I learned how to open my door quietly (because it made a pop sound every time I opened it), and I hid in the front hall closet if he came out while I was moving about. If I was near a heating and air vent, I would listen to what was being said. Voices traveled, and the vents served as my listening agent. Early on, we had an intercom system in the house, and that also was a tool I used to see if he was angry or would abuse my mother.

At this point, every negative word hung around my neck like an albatross. There was this coward, my third-grade teacher, whose words stung and stuck. One day my desk was cluttered with paper because I kept everything. I didn't throw anything away. I felt attached to everything that I owned. I could always look at my work or any of my possessions and feel ownership and relationship. Tossing my work or drawings made me feel as if I was being abandoned. My teacher yelled at me because I did not take my papers and drawings home. She said that I would not be more than that cluttered desk and that I would be nothing in life. She was mean to me and nice to the other children. I felt she never liked me; therefore, did not know or care that my cluttered little desk was the result of my cluttered mind, longing for help. She was so cruel, and she unknowingly acted as an agent of oppression, and so I went through my elementary school years with these words eating away at my self-esteem and my self-worth.

Buffer

During the process of my healing, the Lord spoke to me one day while I was brushing my teeth. He said, "You are a charmer." With pasty foam in my mouth, I looked up at the mirror and said to my reflection, "Charmer? No, not me." My mind immediately went to the outward winking of the eye as a common form of charming and flirting. He said, "Let me show you." He reminded me of situations that had produced the charmer from about the time I was a little girl until I was a teen. Charming was what I had used as a buffer between Roscoe and me. When Roscoe was upset or there was a good chance that a beating would take place, my mom always said, "Be nice to your dad. Bring him his food, go give him a hug, and go see if he needs anything in particular." My siblings would also send me to get stuff from Roscoe. When we would go on those long fishing trips, my brothers would put me front and center and say, "Angie, go ask Daddy," even after he had told them no. I would skip my little self-straight up to Roscoe, hug him around his neck and smile, and talk nicely to get something in return. This is where that charming spirit entered in. As I grew older, I began to loathe taking Roscoe his dinner and being nice to him. I thought he was old and disgusting. He began to leer at me, and he became a pervert in my eyes. I began to resent being a buffer.

Living with a Pervert

Roscoe was verbally abusive toward me, and it was demeaning and degrading. He wanted so much obedience and respect from me. It was as if he wanted me to bow down to him. He would tell me that I was going to be fast and end up a prostitute. To my horror and anger, I learned later in life that he was an ex-pimp. As an adult, I was surprised, but in retrospect, I began to understand that when it came to women, his mindset was both controlling and degrading. Eventually it became clear that he was also a pedophile, and he set his sights on me as I developed into a young lady. As I got older—about sixteen—things got progressively worse.

I began to become a very pretty young girl, and he began to make seductive compliments. When I got ready to go out, he would tell me to come through the living room. He would stand there with a Cheshire-cat grin and tell me how nice I looked. His eyes would roam over me, and he'd make a sound like the character on the old Grumbling Bear cartoon as he leered from my legs up to my crotch and finally made eye contact with me. I felt as if he was raping me without even touching me. It was so creepy and disgusting. He never did it when my mom was around. His comments began to scare me, so I started leaving when I knew he was not in the living room, or I would go through the front door so he couldn't see me. I was at the peak of disgust, and the hate that rose up in me seemed to heat up my body to where my vision began to blur. (I didn't know at that time what a pedophile was, but as I profiled Roscoe later in life, I learned that he was truly a pedophile!)

A Silent Cry for HELP

I just could not grasp the thought of this abuse being okay. Did my mother know he called me a prostitute? Did she know how he looked at me? I began drinking after school, but I first tasted the alcohol in the limousines. It was my job to refill the decanters, so it was a little for me and a little for the decanter. I found marijuana and pills in the cars, too. I was smart enough to toss the pills—thank the Lord! — but the marijuana I kept. I thought it would be okay, but after I had smoked it, I decided it wasn't a smart thing to do since it had been left in there by rock stars—we always handled musical stars who had concerts at the Cow Palace in San Francisco. (The Cow Palace was originally a large steel structured arena that initially operated as a place for livestock trading and in its later days held crusades and musical concerts). Looking back, I don't think it was just weed; I had never been so high in my life. Every building seemed to move in slow motion, as I moved slowly, and my speech was messed up. My friend Lucile and I decided to ride the bus in San Francisco, and I got on the 54 Excelsior and lost my memory. Thank God I made it home. I didn't like the marijuana, because it made me too high and vulnerable. So, I left marijuana alone after that, but I just kept drinking, as if that was a better option. When I drank, I could laugh and act silly, but at times, I cried and became angry and violent.

Who Did I Become?

I often wondered why I felt fear, unbelief, doubt, violence, anger, slothfulness, tiredness, nightmares, traumatic dreams, and a lack of self-esteem. I wondered why rejection took such a forefront in my everyday being. The spirit of fear and anxiety resided in me also—fear of being left alone, fear of rejection—along with tormenting dreams and self-seclusion. My days as a child, and even into adulthood, were structured only by what people thought of me, what I was told by someone else that I could or could not do. I had no self-will or drive, no ability to externally organize the creativity I had on the inside. The spirit of heaviness convinced me daily to suppress my mind. It told me, "They won't accept you," so I suppressed myself and lived in my subconscious mind, never living out what I envisioned myself to be. I enjoyed the thoughts of doing things like being a nurse, creating and designing, and simply playing the tambourine. I was always creating in my head, but I never actually stepped forth and acted on my thoughts. I never raised my hand or participated in school. I would think the answer, and when someone would say what I said in my head, I was more than satisfied. I did not have the ability to compliment myself, to say "I'm an okay person" or "I like me." I always hid my body and downplayed my facial features and my curves because they made me feel trashy. To me, they were an indicator that I would become the prostitute that Roscoe had told me I would become. If I was congratulated for anything, I thought I was unworthy of the compliment. My mother always told me how beautiful I was, but beauty had never gotten me the love I longed for. I was the fat girl with the pretty face. I didn't want to be the fat girl, so I struggled for many years with bulimia and just about every diet in American history. I hated my shape, my huge thighs, my hips, and my large triceps. I loathed them, and I sank deeper into my despair.

Emotional Heaviness

A heaviness consisting of depression, low self-worth, rejection, and bitterness had taken control of me and signed a long-term lease on me without my approval. I did not have the ability to be out front—a leader. I was withdrawn and aloof, cringing and shrinking when someone stared at me. I hid behind my imaginary wall as if I were not living in the reality of the world. I made myself a hermit secluded from others and resolved myself to being alone. I hated to hear arguments or fighting; it made me cringe. I was always nervous in a crowd and was afraid of meeting new people because, in my mind, I would not be accepted. I struggled with normal everyday living and was deprived of what I believed was the normal life I deserved as a child.

I was always told how beautiful I was on the outside. The shocked responses I got when I admitted to having low self-worth was often hilarious. But people were basing their opinion on my chiseled features, on the superficiality of beauty. But was I told I would be a great woman of God, or a successful nurse, lawyer, or doctor. These people didn't say to me, "You have a bright future ahead of you, and you will be wonderful at whatever you set your mind to do. Just how I looked? I just knew that I desired to become somebody in life. I only dreamed about having a happy, abuse-free family.

Change, or So I Thought

One afternoon in 1984, there was a familiar face in my home. I was taken aback because we never had company, and I recognized this man from our picture album. He was the man in the picture with Flip Wilson and Roscoe. He was sitting on the sofa when I got home from school. Everything was quiet and strange. I said a quick hello and went to my room. A few Sundays later, my mom told me we were going to church. I was shocked because I always went to church alone, to the San Francisco Christian Center where Bishop Green presided. I loved being at church—it was my place of peace.

It turned out that the man was an old friend of Roscoe who was now an Elder at his church. Elder Callows came to our home and reached out to Roscoe with the word of *salvation*. Roscoe had played the jazz music scene in San Francisco's Fillmore district in the early '50s and '60s. Despite his demons, he had a love for jazz music. He was a self-taught musician. He couldn't read music, but he knew it by ear. He could play the organ and did it very well. He had old, classic vinyl records of old jazz artists. At that time, anything he liked, I hated. However, I did love to listen to Johnny Mathis and Donnie Hathaway, and I would sing their songs all the time. I also loved every note Ella Fitzgerald even whispered. On a good note, Roscoe sent us to music school and insisted that we also had to learn to play golf and chess. We practiced daily as a part of our chores. When we were all in the home, we all played an instrument—violin, soprano sax, bass guitar, and two of us played the organ. Roscoe's intentions were good, but his mental imbalance did not allow us to enjoy a peaceful life.

The new church life was not long-lived. It lasted for a short while, and in that time, I did not encounter a violent outbreak in the home. But that suddenly changed. Roscoe was still the abuser he had been when we left for church, and he was still the same when we got home. There was no change in him.

He will genuinely attempt to convince the partner that the abuse will not happen again and even agree to go to counseling.

Time was moving on, and somehow my mother convinced Roscoe to go to counseling at the church. Unfortunately, this made life at home worse. My mom would be abused for what she talked about in counseling. I just wanted her to take a baseball bat and let Roscoe have it once and for all. After so many years of abuse, my mom had become very distant and reserved but still very kind. She began to drink more and more. Some of the arguments were about me—Roscoe would "go off" on my mother about my bad attitude. And it had gotten worse. As my anger kindled, I had become silently aggressive. I was not verbally responsive, and my silence and heartfelt loathing of Roscoe was getting to him. During this time, I noticed a strange emotional shift in the atmosphere of my household. I recall having a very bad attitude and my mother said to me that she was tired of my attitude and asked if I wanted to go and live with my sister. My heart screamed, "Hello? Can you please try and find out why I am this way?!" And then I thought, *"Are you really going to send me away to her? Does she want me to live with a person I don't even know? "Someone who treated me so badly?"* I was beyond broken. My mother was all that I had, and now she wanted me to go away?

Children who are exposed to battering never feel safe. They are always worried for themselves, their mother, and their siblings.

She didn't realize that she ripped my heart out that day. I had no one, and I had nowhere to go. I began to think that Roscoe was going to kill her and wanted me to go away so that he could do it. I decided not to go away to college because I felt like I had to stay to protect her. Did she want to get rid of me for *him?* Or was she trying to protect me? The rejection piled on yet another layer, and it made me even angrier. Some days I didn't even go to school. I just drove around in my Seville until it was time to come home. I was beyond confused; I was now despondent.

Our Way Out

Things began to get worse. I started seeing Roscoe drive up and down the street by my high school. Everyone knew us because of the limo business, and my friends would tell me, "I saw your father. He was waving at me." One particular girl seemed disturbed and stated that she had seen Roscoe also. She said, "He always waves at me, but I don't know him. Why does he wave at me like that?" I could say nothing, but I began to feel as if he was plotting to harm one of my friends in some way. I had a nasty feeling about it, and I was embarrassed because they knew, and I knew why he was waving.

I vacillated between the fear of being molested and the fear of killing Roscoe if he tried. One Saturday morning in 1986, I was awakened by another abusive moment. I heard intense arguing and threats of violence. It was worse than I had heard before. The pounding of her face began, and I could hear the slaps and screams. Then he began to choke her. I heard my mother gagging. I was so scared. I opened my room door, and it just came out—I screamed, "STOP! Leave her alone!" I began to walk toward my mom, screaming, "STOP choking her!" He let her go and hit me so hard that it knocked me out cold! All I remember is going down. I knew I had a concussion because I had no memory of the remainder of that day. I don't remember hitting the floor. I knew I was going down, but by the time I hit the floor, I blacked out. The next day when I realized what had happened, I was enraged. Thoughts of murder entered my mind. Neither my mom nor Roscoe ever discussed the incident with me. Life just went on.

A Spirit of Revenge

Most experts believe that children who are raised in abusive homes learn that violence is an effective way to resolve conflicts and problems.

I woke up from the blow as a different person and began to plot the killing of Roscoe. I knew where his .38 revolver was and had a mind to use it, but thought it would overpower me. One day, I went into the garage looking for something to kill him with. I didn't know when I was going to do it, but I remember that I did not have an ounce of fear anymore. I found an old steel gas pipe and placed it in my closet. When was I going to do it? When he fell asleep on the couch watching those stupid four-hour westerns? I knew I had to do it in one blow. I vividly remember saying to myself that if he came in my room or even attempted to touch me that I would have to kill him. I would look Roscoe in the eye, which I hadn't done before, and I would not say one word to him. I would stare him down and roll my eyes. I hated him with a passion and was ready to do to him what he had done to me. I knew he understood that something had changed in me. He began to be overly nice and offered to buy me things, which was the norm.

Explosive behavior and moodiness, which can shift quickly to congeniality, are typical of people who beat their partners.

I thought that his buying me something was payment for abuse. I just knew in my heart that he was going to kill my mother and me. I thought again about the .38 revolver in the bottom armoire drawer and thought he was going to kill us with it. If I had to, I would kill him first.

Fortunately, Roscoe's knocking me out cold must have been my mother's breaking point, because not long after the incident, my mother left Roscoe and divorced him. Former friends of the family stated that Roscoe had found the pipe in my room and he feared that I was trying to kill him. Well, at that point, I was glad he got the picture. But I'm thankful to God that I did not go through with it.

I never told anyone at church what went on in my home, even after the divorce. I was told by one of Roscoe's close friends from church that I should apologize to him because I didn't want the fact that I treated him so badly on my conscience. *Say what?* This man persecuted us and then told our former church so many lies. I could not believe that his lies were perceived as truth! But my mind was programmed to keep the horror to myself. I quite frankly never even thought about telling anyone, because it was so embedded in me never to tell anyone what went on in our home.

Real Talk: It's very unfortunate that the spirit of control lingers long after you're free. My research revealed that a man or woman who wants to control and contain will place fear boundaries on you, and when this is done, even though you have an opportunity to break free, you won't. What shocks me about myself is that I did not have the mindset to tell, but only to survive in my home by learning my enemy well.

Secrets

When I was seventeen I found out that Roscoe was not my natural father. I had never been told that. Not until my mom left him for good.

You mean to tell me this fool wasn't even my daddy? That knowledge didn't help me at all. I was happy, and I was mad. And now I was digging deep, trying to find out who I was and what the heck was going on. I wanted to know who my daddy was and where in the world was he. My heart got happy for a moment when I thought he could protect me and that I could go live with him. I wanted to meet him. Here was yet another blow. My mother told me that my biological father, Benjamin Harvey Holmes, was killed before I was born. My mom was just a few months pregnant with me, and she already had four children. Oh, how devastating! I couldn't even imagine the fear, loneliness, and mental anguish she endured.

It got even more complicated. Interestingly enough, my natural father's family resided in the same cities that I did— Daly City and San Francisco—and I never knew until I was an adult that they were so close! I even went to school with my cousins, ironically finding out in our adulthood that we were related. As an adult, my anger resurfaced. I was angry when I learned that I'd had a family I wasn't allowed to know or see. All that time, I could have left. All that time, I had somewhere to go. I always knew I was different, but I never knew why. I couldn't understand why I had to endure the abuse, and I was very angry with my mom.

At this point, I spiraled out of control.

Children from violent homes have higher risks of alcohol/drug abuse, post-traumatic stress disorder, and juvenile delinquency.

It was 1987, and we now lived in Berkeley, California and I had some major battles warring within me. I had opened myself up to too much too soon. I met my first real boyfriend in my school parking lot. This guy had something about him, and I was captivated. I was drawn in, and I recognized his spirit in a way and felt so attached to him. Oh my, was I in love! This was a feeling I had never felt before. He took me to school, to the movies, to the park, and even dropped me off at church on youth nights—wherever and whatever I wanted, he did it. He even let me wear his leather letterman jacket! Ladies, you know when you get the coat, it's serious! It was a Fairytale getting ready to unfold. He was very smooth, and he wanted to know where I was all the time. I thought that was cute. I felt as if someone finally cared about me. Ray had this dominance I was so attracted to. There were times he would just show up at my mom's house without me knowing. I would get home and be shocked to see him sitting and talking to my mother, and I thought, "Well, alright then; this is definitely going to lead to marriage." Before I met him, I was working my looks and charm to get into clubs at eighteen. I knew the bodyguards, the police officers, and, of course, all the bartenders. I was eighteen, and I knew I was fine. By this time, I was deep into bulimia. I was sick and weak, but it kept me at 5'2" and about 125 pounds with a tiny waist and I was happy.

My New "Boyfriend"

Ray started going to the clubs with me. The men I knew still spoke to me, hugged me and bought me drinks. He did not like this and made it known by a subtle, but firm and noticeable squeeze of my arm. The first time he did it, I flinched and asked what was wrong. He had a look on his face that I hadn't seen before. My girls started to notice that every time we went out, he showed up. "What's up with that?" they asked. I just responded by saying, "Girl, he's sprung!" and we giggled and slapped five. Little did I know, he was stalking me.

One unforgettable Saturday night at the Palladium in San Francisco, Ray suddenly appeared. We were on the floor dancing and raising the roof. The Palladium was one of those clubs that had no room to walk—it was always packed, a real fire hazard. My girl screamed in my ear, "He's here!" I looked toward the stairs at the far back wall, and she was right. Ray stood there with a cold, straight face, hands in his pockets, and stared. How in the heck he saw me in that thick, dark, jam-packed crowd was anyone's guess. If you've ever been to the Palladium, you know what I'm talking about. I made my way over to Ray. He looked me dead in the eyes and told me it was time to leave. When I said we'd just gotten there, he told me slowly and firmly, "You're leaving now." He walked closer to me, got nose to nose with me, and I felt a little fear, but like a fool, I left with him.

I walked up the stairs to leave the club, and he followed close behind me. I could feel his anger tingling the hairs on the back of my neck. As we approached his car, Ray opened the door for me as he always did, and I got in. By this time, my heart was racing. I asked Ray where we were going, and he didn't respond. Ray took me to his house and locked me in his room. Without warning, he wrapped his hand around the front of my neck and under my chin so tightly that I was on my tiptoes trying to loosen his grip. He began to yell and ask me what I thought I was doing dancing with other men. By this time, I was crying and begging him to let me go. He finally did.

Falling prey to an abuser has nothing to do with a person's intelligence. Vulnerability and self-esteem issues that often stem from childhood are common reasons people are attracted to abusive relationships.

I did not remember that Ray had locked his door from the inside with a key. I ran to the door and couldn't get out. He grabbed me by the neck again and began to say, "You know I love you!" He just kept telling me he loved me; then threw me into his closet and shut the door. I was a wreck, and I was afraid to fight back. When Ray opened the closet door, he had a stun gun in his hand. I begged him not to use it, but he kept coming towards me, threatening me with it. I did what I knew and had learned to do to men, which is turn on the charm. I began to tell him I was sorry and that I would never do it again. I said I didn't realize he loved me so much He was a totally different person the next day, and I began to make excuses in my mind for what happened. One part of me said, "He's psycho and, girl, you better run," but the other side said, "It's not his fault, it's yours—somebody finally loves you, and you disregard them. Angie, you're stupid for messing up again. Yes, I know you are probably saying, "*WHAT?!*" But remember, it was a learned response for me. It was the only kind of love I had experienced from my parents and the only kind of love I could relate to. To make matters worse…Ready for this? My boyfriend's father physically abused his mother and, unfortunately, I knew this from the beginning and never gave it a second thought. I thought the abuse was love.

As time went on, he flashed on me many times, and just as I had with my stepfather, I learned how to stay safe. Ray would do subtle things to me in public places when he was angry with me or if he thought a guy looked at me or vice versa. He would pinch me, or squeeze my arm, or grab the back of my hair like he was caressing me and pull it. Sadly, I loved him. I really loved this guy. I didn't like what he did, but I loved Ray as a person, and I couldn't stop seeing him no matter what he did. (Déjà-vu, right?) I felt comfortable and never wanted to be apart from him. In many ways, he was like my stepfather. This was an illness! I had no desire to separate from him, and I felt that he was right and I was wrong, and I was the one who caused the abuse. The words of my stepfather were coming true!

Then things ended abruptly; glory to God! I showed up at Ray's house, and he wouldn't let me in. I asked him why, and I immediately knew it was another woman. I was furious! My heart was racing, and I felt my throat start to close up. *This is not happening! How could he, and why is he doing this to me?* My heart was crushed, and I cried all the way home. Of course, when he called, I answered his phone call. I was waiting for it. I had no self-worth or self-esteem. I was half crazy myself, and again, I didn't know any better. No matter how much I loathed my stepfather and his abuse, I was unknowingly attracted to it. My boyfriend kept cheating, and I kept crying. What I thought was love was not love at all. It just was my emotions wanting to be fed what it was used to. After the break-up, I became physically sick, crying for days. I secluded myself and turned into a crying drunk. I was torn, hurt, and depressed. Music always seemed to depict love in some sort of way— either good or bad— and I found solitude in a group called Jodeci. I played their tape day and night until it broke.

I let go of what little boundaries I had left, and I went on a downward spiral. I began to drink alcohol until I blacked out. I became an alcoholic. I went to clubs from Monday to Sunday—The Palladium, Club Townsend, Oakland Army Base, Solar System, The 49ers Club, and even some raunchy after-hours spots in Oakland. Every day of the week, we found a club to go to. Somehow, I got my hands on a pink, pearl-handled .22 automatic, and we did not club without it. I would still go to youth night on Friday nights, but then I'd head to the club after church. Only God's mercy kept me. I began to live an unfruitful and unhealthy life with drug dealers and night clubs. I was riding a wave that seemed never to hit shore. It would be weeks at a time before my family would hear from me. I needed help and healing because I was far from God. My past had become heavy baggage which got heavier every day.

Mercy said NO!

In September of 1989, in one of my drunken states, I made the awful mistake of driving home after the club. The girls and I created this drink called "purple" which was a toxic, deadly concoction of alcohols. While driving and trying to make my way to the Bay Bridge, I blacked out and lost consciousness from the alcohol. I hit a twenty-foot wooden utility pole, and it fell on my car right down the middle of it. I still did not wake up! When I did become conscious, the car was bowed, and the doors were jammed due to the frame being crushed. The pole was inches from my head, right on the side of my face. I tried to look over to see if my friend was okay, but I could barely see her, so I called her name. She was unconscious from the alcohol too. After desperately waking her, we made our way out of the car alive, without a scratch. I had crashed drunk and woke up drunk. I was so inebriated that I was still drunk well into the afternoon of the next day. I could have died that day, but mercy said NO! I had no way to consciously cry out to the Lord to save me. If that utility pole had fallen three inches to the left, I would be dead. If it had not been for the Lord, my soul would have been lost that night. God held back death and spared my life. If it had been up to the enemy, he would have had my soul that night.

Unfortunately, this event did not change things. I continued in this dismal state of mind without receiving the healing that my mind or soul needed. I just went on with life, looking for something to pacify my longing and brokenness. I was left desperate, broken, and hopeless.

CHAPTER TWO: **A PACIFIER**

It was the summer of 1990. I couldn't wait for my twenty-first birthday. My girlfriend had found a new club in San Leandro for us to go to—the 1989 Loma Prieta Earthquake had damaged so much in San Francisco that the Bay Bridge and our usual club spots were closed down, and it took far too long to go across the Golden Gate Bridge. We dressed as fly as possible with matching outfits, of course—black minis with checkered tights and Via Spiga heels, blazers, plenty of gold chains, rings, bracelets, and Gucci purses. We always looked good.

We arrived at the club, and I thought the spot was so weak. *Look at all these young scrubs*, I thought. I had always been attracted to older men. While sitting at the bar, I noticed a guy with a Jheri-curl. I thought his Cazal eyeglasses were fly, and I couldn't tear my eyes away as he tried unsuccessfully to holler at a chick who was brushing him off. I found the whole scene comical.

The night went on, and we left the club. We had to stop for gas and guess who I saw? The Jheri-curl dude with the Cazal glasses! I kept pumping gas and ignored him—I knew how to ignore and still get the attention I really wanted. He asked me if he could talk to me, and we ended up exchanging numbers.

He called me the next day. He said, "Hi. This is James." I said hello as well and waited in silence. He was different, and I thought he was too quiet. He didn't really know what his game was, and he was definitely not the kind of guy I was used to. He seemed safe. I saw how his sisters came to his house and washed his dishes and how his mother told him what to do. She even showed up on our dates—that irritated me so much! Even so, I ignored all of my reservations, and we began dating full force. Not long after that—just a few months—I moved in with James.

This man was different from the other guys I had met and dated—much different. I seemed to lean toward rough and abusive guys—I believed that if a guy was angry with me or verbally or physically abusive, it meant he loved me.

Women who were abused by their fathers most often find themselves desiring and dating abusive men.

A man had to be rough and firm. I needed to feel he was above me. Violent and controlling men appealed to me because they were what I had seen and experienced as I grew up, and my twisted thinking told me that it was how you should feel with a man. This man, to me, appeared to be a reason for me to slow my life down.

During this time, I was so far from God. My heart was empty, I was broken, and I was lost. But I thought of God daily and longed desperately to be back with the Lord. Somewhere along the way, I had let condemnation set in. I had accepted what the enemy said instead of God's Word. I tried to make my life make sense, but I couldn't. I felt out of place outside of Christ. I knew that I belonged to God, though in my mind, I knew that one day, I would give my life back to Him. I just didn't know when that one day would be. The enemy had my mind tangled and lost; and presented a false picture of peace before me. I was suffering from the residuals of a dysfunctional family life, and Post Traumatic Stress Disorder (PTSD) and anything that seemed peaceful was welcomed without question.

Remember, I had recently broken up with a boyfriend who I'd thought I was desperately in love with, and I didn't know how I would ever recover. But there was James, who drove an old Seville—the boxy kind. He had a Jheri-curl, big eyes, glasses, and was pigeon-toed. I was excited. I didn't use drugs, but I smoked a few joints here and there. And alcohol, a family favorite, was one of my top choices. I stayed drunk as often as I could. I never found peace and contentment from it. In reality, the peace that would satisfy my longing was in God. It was my soul longing to be free and satisfied in my Savior, not by a man. I needed God, the only one who could caress and heal, the only one who knew my every groan and could comfort me. But decided I had found what I needed in James. He was my only hope and idea of some sort of life. The more time I spent with James, the more I began to need him, but I was still empty. As time went on, I saw more of his family than mine. I adapted to his friends and saw less of my own. His life had become my world.

Histories Collide

It was the spring of 1995, and I had a very vivid dream. I saw two large hands coming toward me and touching my stomach. Startled, I woke up, knowing I was pregnant. I immediately stopped drinking. My daughter was born that February. She was so beautiful, a creamy tan with straight black hair. When the doctor handed her to me, she was crying. As I caressed her, she opened her eyes, looked at me and stopped crying. My heart melted. Because she brought so much joy to my life, I began to feel like life was worth living now that I had someone to love.

Soon after, I encouraged James to propose to me, and we got married in the fall of 1996. Did you hear what I said? *I encouraged him!* Baby, that was a foolish move. My daughter was born seven months before we got married, and I was so sure this was the right thing to do. I wanted to be married so badly. I wanted to create the opposite of what I had seen and lived as a child. I wanted to love and protect my child and never let anyone hurt her (like I had been). I was passionate about my dream for this ideal family.

While on maternity leave, I couldn't sit in the house another Sunday. I wrestled with bombarding thoughts of giving my life back to Christ, and I found a church to attend, which wasn't far from our home. It wasn't like the church I was used to, but I was in the house of God, and I felt so free. I eventually went back to the church that I had grown up in, so I traveled every Sunday from San Pablo, California to San Francisco, California for church. It bothered my husband, but he didn't tell me not to go. I asked James if he wanted to go with me, but he always said no.

Our ideas of marriage were at the two far ends of the spectrum—he had no clue how to be a husband, and I had abuse and control guiding me as a wife. To add to the craziness, I agreed to allow his mother to live with us. Why did I do that? She didn't like me at all, and there were times when she would just sit and stare at me, and oh, how that irritated me. I stayed in my room most of the time. What a life! It quickly went from bad to worse, and eventually, I convinced James we needed to move and have our own home and privacy. It took James what seemed like months to tell her. Why was he scared to tell his mama that he wanted to move?

I wanted James to take control of our life, our daughter, and plan our future and finances. But James didn't care. It wasn't what was in him at the time, and I was too immature to see it. I was pushing James into a place in which he did not have the capacity to function. I ended up playing the dominant role, and this affected my respect for James. I asked him to go to marriage classes with me, and he went to a few then refused to continue. I gained knowledge about a wife's role and a husband's role in our marriage, and I began to step back.

My hopes and what I had longed for in marriage were diminishing, I didn't know what marriage was supposed to be like. I always thought that because his mother had done so much for James, he thought I was supposed to take on that same role. I thought to myself, *I am not his mama; I'm his wife. He's supposed to take charge, make decisions, and protect.* But instead, he left it to me to make both minor and major decisions, and I was irritated. We were both too immature for marriage. The more James relied on his mother, the more I began to lose respect for James, and the angrier I got.

But I continued to go to church, and the more I went, the more mentally sound I became. As the Lord would have it, the process of my true healing began in 1997. My daughter was a year old, and I gave my life back to Christ. I felt the ton of bricks that were on my shoulders fall off. I was so excited, but when I arrived home, I felt sadness. I knew James would not approve. I remember the day that I told James I had given my life to the Lord—he stared at me, walked out the door and didn't speak to me for weeks!

I knew I had to go back to Christ. I just could not go on with life without Him. The reverence and honor of God were so deeply rooted within me, and the Holy Spirit never turned off. I kept holding on to the scripture verse, "In the same way, you wives, be submissive to your own husbands so that even if any of them are disobedient to the word, they may be won without a word by the behavior of their wives, as they observe your chaste and respectful behavior" (1 Peter 3: 1-2).

Something Is Missing

The number one need of a woman is affection and love, not sex. ~Dr. Myles Munroe

Life for us progressed, and we made it to our ten-year anniversary! In 1999, my first baby boy was born. He was long, skinny, cute, and looked just like his dad. We bought our first home in Vallejo, California. This was a dream and a huge milestone. We progressed financially and were able to do what we wanted when we wanted. Our expectations of each other seemed to balance out, and we began to have a better marriage, or so I thought. We started having a little fun being a family and learning how to be parents. I learned to overlook as most wives do and to suppress my desires. I often told James how I felt like his sister and that I needed affection and caressing. I felt empty, alone, and unloved for the majority of my marriage. I was just too broken inside to be married. Don't get me wrong—I wasn't a perfect peach remember, my understanding of marriage was what I saw growing up. Our relationship seemed okay when I was cursing James out and falling asleep drunk. We were two broken pieces trying to mend ourselves with shattered instructions. Our second son was born in January of 2002.

Life was all about the three children, school, daycare, homework, training, nurturing—and we both worked full time.

It was now 2003, and I started to notice how he wanted me to take the kids with me whenever I left home and how his patience with the children had changed. He began to drop little comments, saying that ever since I was saved, we didn't have much in common. I wondered, *Where is this coming from? That was so long ago.* Yes, some things absolutely did change—I did not drink alcohol like a fish anymore, and I did not curse James out or hang out in clubs, making it home drunk by the next day. Yep, that was the major change. But he began to say I wasn't the woman he married, and I thought, *Well, no, I'm not the woman you married. I'm thirty-four years old now, and a lot has changed in me from that twenty-one-year-old girl you met years ago. Now she's a woman, a wife, and a mother.* But, I didn't catch on.

His shift at his job changed to the swing shift, and we didn't see much of each other except on the weekends. He began hanging out with his friends again, so he said, and leaving me with the kids. He made new friends at work, cheating friends. He described male friends, yet leaving out the new female coworker. When I discussed these coworkers with a friend of mine, I was informed that they cheated on their wives and some have had girlfriends on the side for more than ten years! I thought, "He'll never do that to me, he loves me."

77% of cheating men have a good friend who cheated.

I adapted to the change. Remember all of the heaviness and dysfunction I entered the marriage with? It was still there. It sat on the back shelf but came out in my dreams and my character. I never got any professional help—I suppressed and moved on. Early on, I tried to talk to James about my past, and especially about my stepfather, but he blew me off by changing the subject, so I never brought it up again. By now I had tricked myself into thinking I was happy. But I wasn't. I merely painted a picture of a life and hung it on the wall. I continued attending church—just the children and myself. He said he didn't mind, so I kept going. Very seldom would he join us, and I never pressured James to go to with us. I knew for myself that only God could draw, and all the mothers in the church reminded me that my life would draw James. I rested in that as I began constantly praying for help. I needed God to change me, and yes, I prayed that God would change him, too. I knew our lives could be better, and I was maturing as a woman, wife, and mother—it was obvious we needed help.

Early in 2004, a huge housing boom rolled in and our home grew to $200k in equity. We were ecstatic and set a plan to sell the house and buy a bigger one. We looked all over, bidding on houses to no avail before deciding to look in Sacramento, California. We found a home we both loved, but I felt us growing apart. He stayed away from home more and more, stating that he had to work overtime or to attend events with his friends. I thought nothing of it because his paycheck reflected the extra work. But then he became noticeably distant. He didn't welcome my touch or embrace. I asked James what was wrong, and his response as always "Nothing's wrong."

He Was Planning the Break-Up All Along

In the process of choosing a buyer for our home, he made the statement, "We should keep this house because if we ever broke up, it would be hard to buy another one." I didn't pay attention to the statement when he said it, but was reminded of it when things began to get progressively worse. I noticed a decline in his patience with me and with the children. He began talking about new coworkers that had befriended him. His choice of slang and even the sound of his voice began to change. He began going on trips and outings with the boys—these new so-called coworkers. I asked questions about who they were, and I got descriptions of men—his boys. The "immoral" woman was one of his new co-workers, but he intentionally left her description out. And so, I moved on, not knowing there had been another woman all along.

Let me interject. God warns men of a "strange woman"—translated as an immoral woman. This is how the Bible describes her throughout the book of Proverbs. She is real, and I experienced these Scriptures coming alive. The adulterous woman has no morals. She may even feel that the relationship she's in is blessed by God. The scriptures warn men about her. "A prostitute is a dangerous trap; a promiscuous woman is as dangerous as falling into a narrow well. She hides and waits like a robber, eager to make more men unfaithful" (Proverbs 23:27 NLT). She is on an assignment from hell and traps weak, foolish men in her bosom.

God will not go against his Word; He will only bless what He can allow, and adultery is a sin, not a blessing. A marriage developed from an adulterous relationship is not one blessed by God, but one blessed by man. Here is a brief description of such a woman—she has no morals, her adulterous actions are a part of who she is, she is immoral in more than one way. She is dangerous, and her intent is to get her prey, wipe her mouth, and say, "I've done no wrong." Just a little further on, you will read about her prowl. Many men have walked away from their families believing in lust, not love, for an immoral woman. God hates division in families; the devil knows this, and families are his main target to divide. Read what He says in Proverbs 6:16 (NLT), "There are six things the Lord hates—no, seven things he detests: haughty eyes, a lying tongue, hands that kill the innocent, a heart that plots evil, feet that race to do wrong, a false witness who pours out lies, a person who sows discord in a family."

It was time to sell the house in Vallejo, California, and we had a few months before our new home in Sacramento was completely built. James suggested that we live with his sister. I refused to ever live with his family again, so he stayed with his sister just five minutes from my girlfriend's house where the children and I stayed. Yep, another wrong move. Anyhow, we would see James when he got home from work and on the weekends. Not long after the move, James began saying he was too tired to see us. I knew he worked swing shift, so I didn't protest. On one weekend we went to stay with James, he said he was going out with friends. He was all dressed up and smelled good. He said it was his partner Joe's birthday, and he'd forgotten to tell me about it. So, we stayed there without James, and he returned in the middle of the night. I asked him how he could forget if he knew I was coming over. He just said he was tired of sitting in the house and doing nothing with us. I don't remember thinking that anything was wrong. My mind and heart never went to the idea that there could be another woman. My mind just did not catch it; I truly believed that he was for me and not against me. My bad.

At this time in my life, I was suppressing nightmares. I found myself lonelier than I could have ever imagined. Life wasn't perfect, and I functioned at a subtle level of depression that I continued to ignore. But I intended to make life and marriage work. My place of escape was in my mind, but I'm not sure I knew what happiness was. I did, however, know that my place in life was better than what I had experienced in my childhood.

Sudden Change in His Behavior

"Why be captivated, my son, with an immoral woman, or embrace the breasts of an adulterous woman?"
(Proverbs 5:20 NLT)

We were on our way to do a walk-through of our new home. While driving to Sacramento, James became very rude and distant. He reclined his seat back and didn't speak to me unless I said something to him. When he answered, it was short and nasty. I asked James what in the world was going on with him, and he turned his head and closed his eyes. In 2005, we moved into our new home. It was 3700 square feet and had five bedrooms. My job was restructuring, and he suggested that I become a stay-at-home mom, so I did not take a direct reassignment and began life at home. Well that was strange, right? He knew all along what his intentions were; he knew he would walk out, yet and still, I thought my husband was for me and not against me.

He might make a sudden change in his appearance or grooming habits.

It was around this time that I noticed James dressing a lot better. His personality began to change in a negative and pompous way. I began to suspect that something was wrong, but I never thought it was adultery. I know it may seem dumb, but adultery was far from my mind. I figured I had wrongly done or said something to James—he was the type to shut down and hold grudges, I was too. Not good.

Because of the distance to his job, he told me that some nights he would be staying at his mom's or sister's in San Francisco, and I agreed. Little did I know I was being played big time. When I could express how I felt and how his contempt was affecting me, James often gave varied reasons for his behaviors and actions. He'd say, "You're different. You're not the woman I married." He would even say, "God took you from me." In this statement, I saw his lack of understanding because God did not take me from James. God was, in fact, making me a better wife. I was no longer a drunk, and I had more patience and love. But it was true that I was not the person he had married and thank God for that!

No More Denial

"Let them hold you back from an affair with an immoral woman, from listening to the flattery of an adulterous woman" (Proverbs 7:5 NLT).

It was April of 2005 and James was getting ready for work extra early. He was showering, shaving, and putting himself together really well. And then it finally hit. I said to James, "Why are you looking so good going to work?" He acted as if he didn't hear me, and then his phone rang. I picked it up to take it to him, and he all but dropped the razor and snatched the phone out of my hand. I stood there in shock. *This isn't happening!* "Why did you snatch the phone?" I asked. He said angrily, "Do I check your phone?"

I demanded an answer, and he gave me some cockamamie excuse of exchanging phone numbers with other female co-workers for business purposes. He said he didn't want me to take it the wrong way. I listened, and I accepted it, but deep down inside, I didn't believe it. When he got home, I was waiting for James, and I drilled him. This time, he said it was just a woman that gave him discounts at a store. He told me he'd stop her from calling him. We talked, and he smoothed me over, and like an idiot, I fell for it. I was his wife, who wanted to believe he'd told the truth. *Cheat on me? No way, let me flip my hair away from my eye with my pinky so you can get a better look. Sweetie, it's me Angela, pretty girl, with long hair, hips and a smile.* I know you may be saying I fell for foolish stuff, but I was in my own little world, and I was invincible, too fine to be cheated on.

Everything Is Falling Apart

A few months later while looking at my credit card charges, I found a charge for a hotel in Napa, California, so I called to tell them they had made a mistake. The hotel contested, and I asked for a copy of the bill to verify the signature. I quickly found out that it wasn't a mistake and that my husband had stayed there with a guest. I continued to discount what the clerk said, even asking them to fax me the signed receipt and verify the phone number. They faxed it to me, and it was indeed his signature. But I didn't recognize the phone number or the name of which the room was reserved. It wasn't my name. Demyra? Who was this woman?

While standing at the fax machine looking at his signature, my heart dropped to the floor, and I became sick to my stomach. Tears welled in my eyes, and my hands began to tremble uncontrollably. I gasped and kept swallowing my saliva. I was about to vomit. It turned out he had a second cell phone I knew nothing about. I called the number, and no one answered.

When he got home from work, he was on the phone, smiling and talking low. The kids greeted James, and he was happy and offered to cook dinner. I was in shock. While he cooked, I went to my room and sat in my chair and cried. I prayed. *What do I do? Father, please don't let it be so!* Later that night, I asked James about the bill. He denied going to Napa, California, so I showed him the fax. He stared at it for a long time. I said nothing, and he just sat there, quiet. He put his hands over his face and began to cry. He said he'd tried to give me everything that he possibly could, and he'd had sex with her and regretted it. Then he said he'd sold his soul to the devil to try to be the best husband and father he could. I fell for the tears and the sob story and cried with James. We talked about moving on, putting it in the past, and raising our children. James said she was a coworker. He became friends with her and had no intention of having a sexual relationship with her—it just happened. But all the time, I wondered, *who is she who has this much power over you?*

"To keep thee from the evil woman, from the flattery of the tongue of a strange woman"
(Proverbs 6:24 KJV).

Lies

May I interject? You plan, plot, and pay for another phone line, a hotel room for you and a woman who is not your wife, and you have sex more than once…and you did not *mean* to do it? It doesn't *just* happen. It's a flirt, drink, a ride here and there, coffee, dinner…and sex! It was a *choice*, not an *accident*.

Now back to my mindset. I really thought he was sincere. I had no reason to believe he wasn't. After all, we had been together at this time for fifteen years and had three small children, right? *Oh God, was I wrong!* He said he would get rid of the phone and the coworker and he wanted to save his family. He said it was just sex, and he didn't love her. *Aww, how sweet.* The battle to try to save my marriage was on, but unfortunately, he was only going through the motions and had no intention of staying. She—the immoral woman—had his emotions and his flesh.

I tried to go on as normal, suppressing the total despair as much as humanly possible. At times, I would break out in trembling cries, and he would have the audacity to get angry and tell me I was crying because I hadn't forgiven him. I didn't even want him to touch me. When he did, his touch and embrace were different. This was not my husband. Who was this? A filthy feeling of disgust would flood me because I kept feeling like he thought I was her. He began to act strangely, almost arrogant, and he would threaten to leave at the drop of a dime. I had nothing and no one because, at this time, I was separated from my family— there was much drama all the way around—and I was at a new ministry where I knew no one. It was the most isolated period of my life, more even than while under Roscoe's rule.

His Foolishness

One night when I was up late waiting for James to come home, the devil was having a field day in my mind. I saw a car drive toward our home, stop, and then start again. I remember saying to myself, "That's my car, and he has stopped to put another phone in the trunk." When James came in and went to sleep, I went outside, looked in the trunk, and there it was another cell phone. And the battery was stored separately from the phone!

Listen! Selfishness without a doubt can break a family apart when one spouse is living for the fulfillment and gratification to satisfy themselves; a workaholic or adulterer can and will shatter other lives, particularly those of their children and spouse, causing others to suffer at the hand of their mistakes.

The devastation I felt was indescribable. My heart was beating so fast I thought it would jump out of my chest. I felt panic and anxiety begin to take my breath away. I turned the phone on and read the text messages. She was thanking James for time he spent with her and telling him how she needed him and loved him. He also had replied the same. They made plans for dates and trips, and details of their encounters and how much they were in love. I was speechless. The dates that he had told me he was hanging with friends or going on a road trip, he had actually spent with her. I began to check my cell phone bill and his secret phone bill. There were multiple calls for over a year. The log showed the date, time, and length of the calls, and I realized that he'd had conversations with her even while he was lying next to me. I dug up old records back to 2004. He had been cheating a long time and I hadn't even known it. I showed James the bills and asked about the number. He claimed he didn't know it, so I called the number and she, the strange woman, answered and said she didn't know him. Well, it turned out that James had been living a secret life, taking her on trips and staying nights away from home with her, using valid excuses and his sisters as a decoy. It hurt, and I was devastated. After I had confronted James again about the evidence, I'd found, again he said he would stop seeing her, but he didn't. It seemed like he felt relieved. He no longer had to hide. This was his way out.

Then It Happened...

Things took a turn after a few weeks. James had the cold boldness to say that he would *not* stop being friends with her and he *could not* just cut her off. He looked at me with great concern while on his laptop and said, "What about her feelings?" "Oh, my; oh, oh what did you just say?" I stuttered—and I don't have a stuttering issue. "You're sick, right?" I grabbed his laptop from him and slammed it on the counter. I was hurt, angry and disgusted at this point.

James began to discount our relationship without regret. He spoke casually of me moving on and finding someone as if he was counseling his sister or a neighbor. He was cold and even laughed and joked about the type of man I should meet. He would then state that he wanted to keep his family, his children, but not me. He'd live in the downstairs bedroom and wouldn't stop seeing her or be friends with her. He said that he had tried, and it just didn't work. He felt as if he was putting his life on hold and missing out on life. Besides, he couldn't hurt her like that. *Seriously?*

It was all so surreal. It was as if my marital situation was a movie, and I was living the lead part! I felt non-existent, worthless, and discounted. He told me to go and find a nice "church guy" and said that he and his coworker had more in common than he and I did—even after fifteen years together! I found myself, curled up in a ball on my closet floor crying uncontrollably because I knew he meant it. He even came into the closet to console me; he rubbed my back and told me that I would be okay. But my biggest fear was true. He said that he was in love with her.

You Become the Enemy

My anger began to turn to rage, and I couldn't stop asking him why. What does she look like? What is it about her that would make you betray me for her? Then James began to compare me to the immoral woman. He talked about how she talked to him—*"For the lips of a strange woman drop as a honeycomb, and her mouth is smoother than oil"* (Proverbs 5:3, NLT). She had a sultry voice just as the Scriptures described, and she supported everything he did. He began to state what she did right, and what I do wrong. I asked James to tell me when I had ever done the opposite of what was right concerning him, and he didn't have an answer. He moved into the downstairs bedroom and began to live with her—and me. I started to notice his subtle dislikes about my body and the way I looked, and he began to tear me down. He asked me to do things and go places that she (the strange woman) enjoyed as if he was seeing her in me and wanted me to be her! The way he held me and touched me felt as if he was handling someone else. He was in essence not with me but with her. I remember feeling his touch and saying to myself, *"Who is this? This isn't my husband."*

Once again, rejection reared its ugly head beyond my mental capacity to deal with it. I was dismayed. He never told me what was truly wrong. He changed his reasons multiple times. When I tried to discuss what had gone so bad that we couldn't work it out, I always got confusing and dishonest answers.

"To deliver thee from the strange woman, even from the stranger which flattereth with her words"
(Proverbs 2:16).

I asked James to at least try to save our marriage, and he agreed to go to counseling. While on my way to meet him there, I reached down to grab something I had dropped in my SUV, and her eyeglasses rolled out. She had been in my

SUV! At counseling, I handed James the eyeglasses. He said, "Thank you. I'll give them to her." *What, did I just hear him say?* During counseling, he sat there and responded as if he was being coached. I think he was doing the counseling just to say he tried and it didn't work. He told the therapist that he had talked to *her* about what he should say in therapy! He went on to say what she did right and what I did wrong. He never once discussed making things right with me and moving on.

The therapist looked at me and said, "He doesn't want this marriage. He wants her."

Face to Face

I still kept trying. It was May 2005, Mother's Day. He gave me a card, and in it, he wrote, *"I'm sorry I can't turn back the hands of time. You were a good wife. I can't change things. I didn't mean to hurt you,"* but he never changed his behavior. He would be gone for three and four days at a time, just to come home and get more clothes.

On Father's Day, June 2005, we celebrated him as we normally did. He looked at me and said, "How can you forgive me? If you had done this to me, I would not forgive you."

But still, I kept trying. When he disappeared, I would meet James at his job and ask James to come home. He'd refuse to and would drop me off at my car and tell me to go home. I would call, but he wouldn't answer, often having his phone turned off. I continued to try to find a way to no avail. I just could not stop fighting for my marriage.

You know, ladies, we can be the best investigators that exist, so I found out who the other woman was. I asked about her and everyone that knew her replied along the lines of, "She's loud, flirtatious, and brash."

"She was the brash, rebellious type, never content to stay at home" (Proverbs 7: 11 NLT).

I went to my husband's job and introduced myself. She flipped. We argued, and it she threatened to have me put out, but I left on my own. After this, I caught up with her again and, unfortunately, got the real truth about their longtime relationship, which at that time spanned more than a year! Again, I confronted James. His reply? "You should have known." Dang, man, you're right. I should have. I was overloaded with adrenaline and fear, with an all-out scream for help in my head. This was a war cry I had learned to perfect in my relationship with God. I had struggled with a lack of family, love, and security, and I married because I wanted a family. I'd had the intense desire to embrace children and parenting with my spouse, but here I was without one.

I Blamed It All on the Other Woman

Placing blame on the other woman without searching myself would not be healthy—it would only mask and pacify my emotions. In my eyes, the other woman had a mission and was on an assignment unleashed by the pits of hell. She unknowingly took the enemy's bait. And it was ultimately my ex-husband's choice to allow her to seduce him away from his family.

"So, she seduced him with her pretty speech and enticed him with her flattery. He followed her at once, like a lamb going to the slaughter. He was like a stag caught in a trap, awaiting the arrow that would pierce its heart. He was like a bird flying into a snare, little knowing it would cost him his life" (Proverbs 7:21 NLT).

Time to Deal with Me

My ex-husband and I were together for fifteen years. I celebrated my twenty-first birthday with James, and now, at thirty-six, I found myself in a place I never imagined. The only way to deal sanely with the demise of my marriage was not to blame others, but to be real with me! I had to see *me* and admit who I was—the broken, dysfunctional person who tried to function without being whole. My proclivities and my depression all played a part in my failed marriage and affected me beyond my wildest dreams. I was in an insurmountable amount of pain, both mentally and physically. I was shocked to realize while in the grieving stage of the loss of my marriage that it was a similar grief to that of death, of losing someone you love, someone close to you. As a wife, you rely on the mental stability of your husband—his leadership, judgment, protection, love, and physical embrace. When all of this is gone, you're suddenly alone, and you must face the pressures of life by yourself. This, coupled with suddenly becoming a single parent, can cause a chaotic mess in your brain. You begin to wonder what you didn't see. What did I overlook? Where and how did it all go wrong? My mind often vacillated between sadness and anger, which was kindled by the fact that he never wanted to discuss our issues, and I never truly knew until the end what he was thinking because he just wouldn't talk to me. Instead, he chose to turn to another woman.

Studies show that separation (legal or otherwise), appears to affect both the sexes in different ways and the psychological effect of these events is immense.

I did not marry to divorce or to look for comfort in another man when things went wrong. We both were far from perfect. I overlooked many flaws and imperfections because we all have them, cleaned up financial messes, and took down just to keep the peace or make him feel better. I said my vows, and I intended to mature, to love, and to live those vows as long as we both lived. I chose to try to develop within marriage, and going outside of my marriage for anything was not an option. I focused on creating what I didn't have. However, the lack of healing and cleansing in me was a subtle hindrance. I needed to be healed not married, but my mindset was to replace what I had lost. I didn't know anything else.

We had both brought a ton of baggage to the marriage, but James, like many men, didn't want to discuss emotional or heartfelt situations. Marriage requires maturity, and if you're committed to it and understand the seriousness of what it means to be married, you will work through the challenges and problems and not run from them.

Marriage is a covenant vow to God and a promise to each other. ~Dr. Myles Munroe

No matter whom you are with, the seemingly resolvable things in life take a small level of maturity to make a decision to deal with them head-on until your desired outcome is evident. However, one does this only if they are passionate and if they embraced the true meaning of marriage and have committed to your covenant vows. The relationship must be important enough to hold onto. As women, especially in a marriage, we must be careful to watch as well as pray. It is said that women mature faster than men. We embrace life's emotional changes sometimes with tears, sometimes with laughter, and too often with contention. But we deal with it. We mature and handle our lives in that stage of life. Unfortunately, some men don't. They have a way of dealing with issues that are totally different from women. I found myself maturing, but I found my ex-husband reverting, reaching back to what he felt he had missed as a boy and as a young man. But I didn't realize this until the end.

Help Us!

There were countless days and nights of stories that should have been red flags, but I ignored them and kept going on as if life were normal (just as I had done as a child). I just wanted life to be good. I couldn't imagine that my husband was having an affair! I became aloof and slipped into a place of confusion. My days were spent thinking, "How am I supposed to handle this? I have children. What am I going to do? What about my children, God?" I reached out to everyone I thought could and would help. I wanted someone who had been where I was, but I found none.

We went through months of dealing with whether he was going to stay or not. I allowed the ball to be in his court because I didn't want my children to go through life without their father. I felt he was all we had. I became a very sad person; I cried most of the time, and I stopped eating. I lost 20 pounds in less than a month, and my clothes were falling off of me. The rejection I felt was horrendous. Again, I tried to reconcile. I told James that I forgave him and asked if we could just go on. He agreed with his mouth, but not with his heart.

In the summer of 2005, we took the kids to Disneyland. James's phone rang constantly, and he answered only when he walked ahead of or behind us. He was on the phone with her, with no regard for the children and me. When we returned home, he even tried to embrace me. I was so hurt and torn down that he said he couldn't believe that I had forgiven him and that he would not forgive me if the tables were turned, he said this more than once. Often, he would ask, "If you forgave me, why are you crying?" Finally, he said he could not take my crying anymore. After saying he was sorry and that he never meant to hurt me, James walked out; he left. The door shut and I stood in silence. What James did not realize is that healing takes time; he quit too soon.

> *Journal Entry, 9/10/2005 – The children know that he is gone. How do I answer their questions when I have the same questions? They are scared, I am scared, and I don't know what to do. How could he do this to us? Doesn't he realize what he has done? Lord, bless my children.*

I was alone in a brand new 3700-square-foot home with no job, money, or vision. I cried out to the Lord in bewilderment. In a matter of months, my life had drastically changed from what I thought was secure to the most vulnerable state I had ever had to deal with in my adult life.

It was God and me, and it was time to be shaken, to rebuild, and to be made new. I didn't even try to wrap my mind around the fact that the Lord was helping me through my trials and dark days. All I could think of was the demise of my marriage, the rejection, and yes, the loneliness.

My babies were afraid. This was not happening only to James and me. My children, who at that time were three, six, and nine would often ask, "When is daddy coming home?" and "Why isn't he here?" I put their questions off as much as I could and always redirected the conversation, giving them just enough information to satisfy their curiosity.

Fear of losing both parents is a physiological effect on children of divorce.

I felt unprotected, and the children began to express their fears as well. They wouldn't sleep in their rooms. They all would sleep in my room with me; all four of us curled up in one bed.

Journal Entry, 10/02/2005 – The Lord said through prophecy, "I have taken you to your wits' end. Die with dignity. You will never see this trial again.

When you come up out of this one, you will come up with a new heart."

What about my children? What did I do? How did my body and mind interact and function? I don't know. Night after night, I would wait for the children to fall asleep and then cry out to God to help us. The enemy began to torment me with fear. He knew he had me—it was a heightened sense of fear to the point of torment, and he was relentless with it! At night, I locked and barricaded my bedroom door when we slept. I had to go on with my life somehow…I just didn't know how. I was so lost that I didn't even know which days to put out the trash can. I felt so much pain that it felt like my entire life was being pushed through a birth canal all over again. I had no spirit. I functioned day by day in a hollow state of life.

James' care and concern dwindled. He saw the children about once a month for the next few months. On Christmas 2005, he said he wanted to come by and see the kids. He did, and that was the last time we saw James for a while.

In January 2006, a horrible storm was pounding Northern California—floods and mini-tornadoes were prevalent—and to add to my distress, my longtime friend, depression, grew and overtook me when I realized I couldn't pay the mortgage or the utilities. I didn't have gas for the car, and I was running out of food. I really had no idea what to do.

Could It Really Get Any Worse?

My unemployment and severance pay had run out. My family began to say nasty things about me, and they distanced themselves from me. The word was out that James left me. I didn't know I had so many enemies. I was the ridicule of both families and our so-called friends. I began selling my clothes and some jewelry, and I held a yard sale. I cried and confided in my dearest friend Celestine every step of the way. She did what she could do to help me mentally. She listened and saw me through my bipolar days and nights. She supported and checked on me daily, and she was truly heartbroken about my situation. I thank God for her because I couldn't have made it through without her support. Her husband gave me money for food, and I was so grateful— we were down to only Ramen noodles.

I reached out to my husband's mother and sisters, but they pushed me away. I told his mother that we had not seen James in months and that I had no money for food. Her reply was, "He told me you put him out and won't let him see the kids." *What the heck?* She kept saying my son this, my son that. It was useless!

I continued to lose weight in a very unhealthy way, and I began to stretch everything in my pantry as far as I could. I didn't want to eat because I felt that when I did, I was taking food from my children. I had never been in this position before in my life; I didn't know what was next. I reluctantly reached out to family members for help. The spirit of pride and rejection had gripped me, and I felt ashamed, embarrassed, and helpless. No one could help and I felt trapped. Little did I know, it was supposed to work this way. As odd as it may sound, God had placed me in this wilderness rearrange my mindset and heal my spirit and soul—all for the making of me. My trust and reliance on prayer had to develop. I had to trust and seek God and learn Him as my source. And so, the journey began…

Journal Entry, 2/8/2006 – I heard the Holy Spirit say, "You are a Tower." Hmm…but I don't get it.

In late February 2006, I got a check in the mail from my mother. She said her money was funny and she didn't know why, but she could send me $100.00 a month. I gave $10 in tithes; yes, I still sowed my tithes. I put $10.00 worth of gas in the SUV, paid $10 each on my electric and gas bill, put $16 on my children's school lunch for the month, and bought $54.00 worth of food. I operated like this for three months. I was both desperate and grateful.

Fear, depression, and ugly pride kept me from going to the welfare office. I didn't even know where or how to get food assistance. One day, I decided I needed more food or we wouldn't make it. It was a rainy, wet, and dreary day, and I found the welfare office. I went in and immediately stood out like a sore thumb. People stared at me from the time I walked in and got a number and a form. The clerk was rude and nasty. She asked me a zillion questions about my income and my children's father and then asked if I owned a home. It was way too much, and I began to ask myself, "Why am I here? Whydo I have to do this, God? What are you doing to me?"

I left and walked to my SUV in a daze without an umbrella. I was soaked. I sat in my truck and cried and screamed at the top of my lungs. I banged the steering wheel and sat there for hours. I can't do it, God! The stares and glares and degrading treatment only added to my deteriorating mental state. I allowed pride to beat me out of getting food aid. I went home, and I began to think about what I could do to get money. I thought to myself, "We can't go hungry and I can't let the lights get turned off. I have to stop crying and suck it up and figure out everything I'm going through."

I searched the house and found the rest of my jewelry and was so happy. I gathered my wedding ring, my necklaces, and all of my 24k and 18k gold, and I found a pawn shop and sold it all. I got enough money for food, put gas in the truck and paid for my children's school lunches, but the money soon ran out, and I hadn't yet paid all the utilities. I struggled to buy food and keep the lights on in that 3700-square foot home for three long months, which seemed like an eternity. Only by the grace of God did we make it. I tried over and over to talk to my husband, but he wouldn't take my calls, and he didn't give us any money until we went to court in late April of 2006 and the judge ordered James to pay child support. I was relieved. A month later, I got a minimum wage job at a bank and began the process of getting reinstated with my former employer. Now, the house was going into foreclosure, and I needed to sell it fast. By the way, I still had not released James from my heart.

Journal Entry, 4/14/2006 – We need food. I can't find him, and I have no words to say. Will I ever stop crying? Hurt is a very soft word for how I feel *right now. But I'm down to $35.00, and I have to make it work. The Lord blessed me with a job. I start in two weeks. Thank you, Lord! Bless and heal my children!*

An Ugly Battle

As if all that had already occurred was not enough, James continued to disappear. He was nasty and angry that I had taken him to court for child support. I threatened to divorce James, thinking that he would say, "No, I want my marriage," but instead of changing his behaviors, he simply said okay and told me his heart wasn't with me and he wanted to be with the immoral woman. He said he should never have married me. That really hurt. Did it take him fifteen years to figure that out?

I often struggled to function in my daily life. My sadness turned into anger, but I had to play happy with my children and suppress my rage. I had to depress the bitterness that I felt toward their father. I spent many nights just sitting in the dark, staring at the fireplace or curled up in a ball crying in my closet so the children wouldn't hear me. Sometimes I screamed to let the pressure out and would eventually fall asleep on the floor in my closet. Then I woke up each morning, put on my mask of the happy mommy, and began my day. The Lord began the process of rebuilding me from the inside out. It was time for purification. The wrecking ball was here, and the process was far from easy.

Journal Entry, 4/28/2006 – Tears are flooding my pages. I can barely write. Please, Lord, help. Where are you? I'm not doing too well, God. Please bless my children to come through this. Why should I continue to live? HELP me go on.

I was eventually reinstated with my original employer and had access to my stock. PRAISE GOD! I took out a loan, and I could breathe a little easier.

The fact that widowed/divorced women suffer from varying psychological stressors is often ignored. It has been concluded in multiple studies that such stressors could be harbingers of psychiatric illnesses (e. g. depression, anxiety, and substance dependence).

As time went on, James began to fight me for the children and the home. His lawyer painted an ugly picture of me as an unfit mother and said that my children should go to live with James and his mother. James and his lawyer began a campaign of lies and even asked the children and me to move out of the house so that he and his mother could live there, saying I couldn't afford it. I was described as a liar, a cheat, and a thief. It was a circus! This went on for four years, four years of hell. I eventually sold the home in August 2006, the same month it was due to foreclose. I moved into a two-bedroom, one-bath apartment with my three children. My credit was destroyed, and it was all I could afford at the time. I shared a room with my daughter, and the boys were together.

The daily absence of one parent, while the children are living with the other, creates a very challenging new family circumstance for children to adjust to, and most don't do so well.

Just when I thought things couldn't get worse, they did. My boys began to wet the bed and cry at night. I couldn't take a step and they were clinging to me. I did all I could to hold my mind together. Things didn't go so well in the apartment. I placed some items on my deck, and overnight, we got robbed. I was terrified! My oldest son asked if we could put a chair in front of the door at night. He was scared, and I was a mental wreck. Every night when we got home, he reminded me to put the heavy sofa chair under the door handle, and we slept with all the lights on. It helped us all feel a little safer.

I began to cry out to God in a desperate plea for help, wondering what was going on. Why was this happening to us? We had done nothing wrong—James had done this! The Lord gave me the understanding that when a husband removes himself from the family, it leaves the family vulnerable to all kinds of attacks from the enemy. His presence as a man had been protecting the family. I understood and had to intercede for my children and cover them. If I slept, I would sleep for about three to four hours, and then I was up praying. I had no other outlet. All I knew was that I had to get God's attention. Despite the prayers, I went through waves of despair, shame, embarrassment, and loneliness. I became vengeful and bitter with any and everyone. I saw every woman as the enemy. I had suicidal thoughts, deep despair, and regret. I was so full of fear it caused my heart to beat rapidly, taking my breath away.

Side Fact: *A recent study by the National Institute for Healthcare Research in Rockville, MD indicated that divorced people are three times as likely to commit suicide as people who are married. The Institute says that divorce now ranks as the number one factor linked with suicide rates* *in major US cities, ranking above all other physical, financial, and psychological factors.*

> ***Journal Entry, 11/04/2006 – I cannot explain how hard the last three days have been. I almost gave up on life. I almost quit mentally. The devil told me to drive my car off the causeway, and I could see myself doing it. What purpose is there in living? This is unbearable. I'm so alone. Hurt doesn't even feel like hurt anymore. Why live? I'm still here, but I don't understand so many things. Why is this so hard for me? It seems like I am suffering, and he is free.***

Rock Bottom

My emotions vacillated between depression and suicidal thoughts. Life went on, and I had a work schedule that conflicted with the kids getting to and from school. I had to teach my nine-year-old daughter how to use a cell phone, to walk her six-year-old brother to school, to walk home with other children; lock the door when she got home; call me when she got to school and when she got home from school. I taught her to be responsible with the door key, pull out the lunch I prepared for them, and to do homework until I got there. She turned into a little mommy too fast and it broke my heart. During this time, their father had parenting time and often stated that he would be out of town vacationing or working and couldn't get the kids, so his mother would. I tried to keep life as normal as possible for the children. I made the apartment seem like a fun house and created a new normal for us. Yet, it wasn't supposed to be this way.

I was bitter. It took time for me to realize that I was only as much as I thought I was. I had to make myself think about life and peace. Sometimes I would sit in my chair, put both of my hands on my head, rock back and forth, and talk to myself. I had to fight my own mind. But I suddenly decided not to give up. If I didn't change the way I thought, I would be right on target for ultimate failure and my children would be lost. It was up to me to fight.

Courage to Fight My Thoughts

This was a long, hard battle. And it was the Lord's doing. I screamed and cried. Why would I let a person have so much control over my mind? Did I have a right to give away the gift that God gave me? If Jesus paid the ultimate price for my life, who was I to give up to emotional distress? These emerging thoughts marked a new beginning in my mind. I started on a personal quest, a personal determination to find out why I existed and how I was to become the person God intended me to be. God created me for His glory, and He created me with purpose. I was determined to find purpose and allow it to manifest in my life. If I allowed divorce to be the end of me, then I would willingly cower out of the precious life that the Lord so lovingly prepared for me. *I had to tell myself that my marriage had ended, not my life!*

It has been stated that women invest more in the family, take larger responsibility for the marriage, and therefore see divorce as a greater failure than do men.

I wasn't going back to alcohol, and I wasn't going to get another man. I was determined to make my pain have a purpose. God's promises are too rich, and I had seen them work in my life. I could not let my children down. They didn't deserve this. I was on a mission to have a purposeful life—I just didn't know how. I began to realize that things could be worse. Each day that I woke, I would think to myself, I made it another day. I am alive! Gratefulness began to fill my heart. No matter how badly I was hurting, I was grateful. I would pray, bang on the floor and roll on the floor. I would lay before the Lord. I felt I had to get His attention by any means necessary (although He had heard me the first time that I called on Him). The pain had not yet released me from its grip, but I made myself think as right as I possibly could! I felt bipolar, but I just settled into it and rode the waves of my healing—one day up, the next day down. I thought my life was spiraling out of control, but God had me. He had it all in control.

Journal Entry, 2/10/2009 – Jr. is having the hardest time. Someone in his dad's family said something to him and hurt him. God, You have to help my son. He is so hurt and angry. His little mind cannot understand all of this. He told me that he hates me and that I made his daddy go away. I don't think my heart has anymore pieces that can be broken. I'm so not getting this. GOD HELP US!!!

Journal Entry, 4/13/2009 – I have suffered alone and long. It seems the warfare shifts daily. The attack on my emotions is relentless. As I take four steps forward, the devil pushes me one step back. I'm tired, I'm weak, and I need help. I need prayer, and I need a word for my life. Please, Lord. Sometimes I wonder why I even fight back. I don't

*want to do this. Do you hear me? Why are you so
quiet with me? Your spirit rains on me, but I don't
see the change in my natural life I want. I don't
know what the rain is doing. I want the rain to take
away the pain. People think I'm so strong… why?
I'm not! I'm weak.*

Running from God

It was the Fourth of July weekend in 2009, and I was
more than depressed. I was still fighting suicidal thoughts,
and I was angry at God. I wanted so bad to go to the beach—
Dillon Beach. Dillon, California was my getaway place. So,
I packed up my friend's SUV, the kids, and a few other
friends and headed west for a two-hour drive.

While driving, I was telling God over and over that I
give up, I quit. God, this is too hard. I don't care anymore,
and I don't want to fight for my mind. I don't want to do
anything in your kingdom. I attempted to check out, and I
did everything I could to get my mind off of God.

While at the beach, we enjoyed food, the shore, and
games. We greeted people and chuckled with the families
sitting next to us. It was the end of the day, and my son said
he was cold and wanted to change his clothes. We headed to
the restrooms, and I waited in between the men's and
women's bathrooms. A young mother and her happy little

daughter passed me. The woman and her daughter entered the restroom and quickly came out. As they passed me, the little girl said, "Mommy, why is that woman on the floor?" Her mother replied, "Walk faster. She's not breathing. We have to find help."

Nope, I Quit!

I said, "God, I told you that I quit!" But my body moved toward the restroom like lightning. Once inside, I saw a woman lying lifeless on the floor, pale and not breathing. I tried not to panic. I didn't know CPR, but I immediately got down on the floor and began to pray that the Lord would restore her breath and give her back to her children. I remember the prayer vividly. After praying for what seemed like forever, nothing had happened. I looked at my watch and prayed again, and this time, I said, "God what are you doing? Why did you have me come in here and see this woman if you weren't going to revive her? Father, breathe life into her body and give her back to her children." (How did I know she had children? It was the intercession of the Holy Spirit.) She began to cough, and her eyes began to roll around under her lids. She opened her eyes, and I began to cry. I asked the lady her name, and she replied, "Mary."

Then the woman who had left with the little girl to get help came in with an off-duty paramedic who had been enjoying time at the beach. He asked me how long she had been unconscious, and I told him six minutes from the time I walked in. We asked her who was she with at the beach with, and she said, her voice slurred, that she was with her husband and children. So, I headed to the parking lot and asked every man with children that I could find if he was there with Mary. The last person I asked was her husband. I looked in the back seat of their car and saw two small children waiting for her. I recognized them and was stunned. It was the couple that we had been sitting next to on the beach. I walked back in a daze to look for my son, and he was at our blanket.

I cried myself to sleep that night and asked God to forgive me for being so selfish and thinking only of myself. That night, I had a dream, and the Lord said, "For the gifts and calling of God are without repentance" (Romans 11:29). God said to me, "You thought you were running from me, but I meant for you to be there." Without hesitation, I responded, "Okay God, I surrender!"

CHAPTER THREE: **THE DIVORCE – THE DEATH OF ME**

I had to realize that my marriage ended…not my life.

T he daunting dysfunction of divorce: Divorce relentlessly brings a massive unwanted change into your life and the lives of your children. It affects everyone negatively, no matter their age. The lives of children are adversely affected as they experience the loss of love between their parents. They are witnesses to the breaking of a marital covenant that was not intended to be broken. When parents break their marriage commitment, the children are often forced to adapt to life in two homes with two different lifestyles, morals, and households. A challenging new family culture is created, and life is suddenly not what it was before. This generational dysfunction can be handed down like a bad family recipe if it is not stopped and destroyed.

It was January 2010, and I had a court date to divide our assets. It was really happening. The assets were divided, and the judge signed the order of divorce in March 2010. It was final; I was divorced, but I didn't feel better. I felt even more detached. I was single—something I had never wanted to be. I spent all of 2010 relentlessly seeking the Lord for order and guidance in my life.

"For the Lord has called you like a woman forsaken, grieved in spirit, and heart sore—even a wife [wooed and won] in youth, when she is [later] refused and scorned" (Isaiah 54:6, AMP).

The Lord knows all too well the pain felt by a rejected wife, and truly, the detachment is real. How fortuitous for the Lord to speak of this type of pain in the Word of God. The pain is but for a moment, but it is real.

Finding emotional mastery is the key to your survival *~Angela D. Holmes*

Facing My Fears

A family is what I had dreamed of and created in my head. I created the family I didn't have growing up, the one I felt that I was supposed to have. My dysfunctional past had sent me on a hunt for my ideal family, and I had embraced a delusional image of happiness based on my desire to be truly happy. It was clear in my mind—a husband and wife with children and no abuse! I was determined to have that. What

I didn't realize was that my dysfunctional history and the fact that I had not been healed had caused me to enter into a marital covenant prematurely. I've often heard women say that divorce is harder than the sorrows of death. I never understood that until I lived it. Fear of being alone became my reality. Most divorcées would tell you that after the smoke has cleared and their brains were able to function with intent and they were no longer on autopilot, they were better in the end than the beginning, even though the road may have been hard, long, and threatening. However, the real battle began when you received your divorce decree. It was then that it became real. Now the battle to come out of autopilot and survive is paramount. God's Word and prayer were the only strength that carried me through my divorce. The Bible gives an explanation as to what the Word of God is intended to do in our lives.

Hebrews 4:12 says, "For the Word that God speaks is alive and full of power [making it active, operative, energizing, and effective]; it is sharper than any two-edged sword, penetrating to the dividing line of the breath of life (soul) and [the immortal] spirit, and of joints and marrow [of the deepest parts of our nature], exposing and sifting and analyzing and judging the very thoughts and purposes of the heart."

The Word is always working even when we think it's not. In time, the power and intent of God's Word will fulfill what it was meant to do in your life, ready or not. I soon learned that the betrayal, adultery, and ultimate divorce were not about James at all, but about me. God was after me; after my heart. It was a time of purification. This may be a large pill to swallow, but God is perfect in all His ways. He has perfect knowledge of us and knows what it will take to make, cleanse, purge, and perfect you and me.

Psalm 139:3 says, "You sift and search out my path and my lying down, and you are acquainted with all my ways." The pain I had endured brought purpose and God was the source of my healing. God's perfect purpose and intended plan for my life had not changed. I was the one who got off course, not God. It may not have been my ideal course, but because God chose me, nothing happened by pure happen-stance. I often wondered what would have happened if I had not made all the dumb moves that caused so many delays in my life. What would I have become?

A Breaking Point

Finding emotional mastery is the key to your survival. Let's deal with what's real. Divorce was a major disconnect and splitting of the road; a junction not intended and not visualized anywhere in my future. My personal experience changed my perspective on the intense immeasurable confusion and pain divorce caused. Marriage is spiritual, and it depicts our relationship with the Lord. This is a fact whether you are a Christian or not. It is an institution designed by God, designed to bring together a single man and a single woman and make them one. A marriage where a man and woman are brought together by force, through adultery, or by sale is not God's order. Even though friends and family may support the couple's desire, and the two stand before God and profess their unity before Him, God's order can never be impure or defiled. God will never bless something that is against His order, and adultery resulting in marriage cannot and will never be blessed by God. It's just not of God. My brokenness was not brought on by the divorce—it already existed and resided unauthorized in my soul.

Life Lesson: Yes; God hates divorce, but He loves you more. God hates what it does to a family. He does not hate the person that is divorced. God is merciful, kind and forgiving. Divorce brings major emotional stages that we were not created for, and these stages can negatively affect your children and your life. Divorce can be dangerous; it makes you fight to survive as you swim through the consequences of your decisions and actions. There are stages of shock, denial, and hope for restoration. There is grieving, there is anger, and there is a true sense of loss. Your emotions will rollercoaster, but this is not the time to lay down and cry. Even if you don't know what to do, start with accepting what is real. Move forward and let go of who hurt you and how they hurt you. God is so faithful and just. He wants us to be successful, and He will not let us become less than His intended purpose for our lives. His love is everlasting, and nothing can change that, not even divorce.

This crisis has brought you a sense of defeat, danger, and fear, but don't forget that it has also brought you opportunity—an opportunity to thrive, create, build, and embrace your healthy future. You have a grave responsibility to yourself and your children. You can choose to act upon this circumstance negatively or positively. We have the free will to make a calculated response or react out of fear, which will bring failure. Responding is a thoughtful, premeditated, calculated move. Responding gives you a heightened success rate and brings you victory. But simply reacting does not.

We are all faced with challenges, trials, and tests with many variations (divorce, recovery from some form of abuse, loss of life, loss of finances, addictions, declining health, or wayward children). Let's relate this issue to a card game. This is the hand you were dealt. Do you throw in the hand, or will you accept the discomfort of being in a position that you have no control over? You can't see your next move, so do you play the hand you have been dealt? I say play the hand and play it to its fullest! Every situation can and will work to your benefit if you allow it. Stay the course and become victory-oriented. You have been given an opportune moment in your life to subdue, dominate, and govern. Ask yourself, "Have I allowed this temporary discomfort to weaken and puncture the very strength I was created with?" Take the free gifts of life, strength, tenacity, critical thinking, independence, and the ability to resist the residuals of life's challenges and turn them into "life lessons" that will cause you to teach, impact, empower, and change. Be selfless enough to help someone else through it. Every pain has a purpose, and every purpose will have challenges to bring your God-given purpose to fruition. You could always fold— it's really all on you. The Book of Ephesians says to redeem the time, make the most out of every opportunity that we have, and live on purpose.

You have dealt with a lot, and your victory will come when you see yourself in a prime position of growth, not defeat. This is a crucial place. Wake every morning with the intent to become a spiritual weapon of mass destruction to the enemy and destroy everything he's touched in your life. When you're healing, perspective is everything. Don't take the strength that this situation is building in you lightly. It has a purpose too.

He Married Her (The Immoral Woman)

Oh yes, it does happen. More often than not, your cleansing will take further steps and require a deeper cleansing. As for me, God knew what still resided down in my soul. He had predestined and foreordained my purpose and would not allow the enemy to have a foothold on any part of me. The Holy Scriptures say that all things will work together for my good. I could not identify the emotions I felt—this was all new. I did not like what I felt, and I needed clarity. What I did not realize was that a emotional connection to my ex-husband still existed, and this is what I was feeling. Healing comes in layers, and up to this point, the remaining layers were deeply rooted. God knew I could not live a healthy, whole life on purpose with residual emotional ties. And so, I started the next layer of cleansing. I did not recognize it at first, but as I became very honest with myself, I realized that God was using the very thing I was praying against to heal me and make me into the vessel that I was created to be.

Journal Entry, 3/1/2012 – "Mommy, Daddy is getting married in Vegas!" Now, I know good and well it couldn't be to her. He told me he would never marry her, that she was not marriage material. He's such a fraud. Another pathetic lie to smooth me over; such a coward.

Journal Entry, 4/24/2012 – Horrible day! Oh my mind; this is an unbearable day. I can't even do my job. I feel cold and stale. I don't like the mental attack. I need help with my mind. I feel like I am losing it again. What did I miss? I thought I was healed!

Journal Entry, 5/3/2012 – I saw the ex-today with no anxiety or fear. He was pleasant and not a jerk as usual. I even congratulated James on his engagement. His hands were trembling, and he stuttered, "Thanks." His look was one of bewilderment. I came in the house and prayed and thanked God for growth. I prayed for his salvation and hers. I can only congratulate James. Why should I hate? I plan to win at all costs. I have enough to deal with—life, kids, everything is on me, everything! I wish I could exhale, but I can't. I must heal, and I must locate this enemy in me that is pressing me.

Journal Entry, 5/5/2012 – Lord, you keep repeating, "Do good to your enemy." Okay, God, You are pressing me. I will buy them a wedding gift.

Journal Entry, 5/6/2012 – I searched until I found the perfect wedding card, and I bought them a wedding gift; a book of prayers for couples. I will drop it in the mail. How does this make me feel? I'm blank right now. I can't stand this bipolar stuff. I think I have a mental problem…is this Angie?

Now Let's Deal

When you stay in the process, everything you need to be and what He has purposed you to be will manifest at the end of the process. ~ Dr. Tamara Bennett

Truths:

1) This was not meant to destroy you, but only to strengthen you.

2) This crisis has brought you a sense of defeat, anger, and fear; however, don't miss that it has also brought you the opportunity!

3) Identify your greatest weakness, and you will find that to be your greatest test.

4) When you know your worth, it becomes difficult to lay down and die.

5) Meditate on your intended outcome according to the Word of God.

Notes: Write down what you are determined to change in your life, based on these truths.

1. _____

_____

2. _____

_____

3. _____

_____

4. _____

_____

5. _____

_____

6. _____

_____

Daily Affirmations – Speak daily with belief, passion, and energy. Digest each word until it becomes your truth.

1) God is not against me; He is for me (Psalm 56:9).
2) I am forgiven and redeemed (Ephesians 1:7).
3) My healing is inevitable; God has healed my heart and my wounds (Psalm 147:3).
4) I am not condemned by God (Romans 8:21).
5) I am chosen and loved by God (1 Thessalonians 1:4).
6) I will prosper and succeed (Jeremiah 29:11).

Prayer: *Father, thank you for working purpose in our lives and being acquainted with our grief. Thank you for your perfect plan to cleanse, heal, and make us whole and fit for your divine use. We accept your will for our life. Please give us instructions to move forward. In Jesus' name, Amen.*

PART TWO |
INTERNAL COMPONENTS

CHAPTER FOUR:

TOO HEAVY TO HOLD

Heaviness (Heavy) – a continual weight, having great weight; a heavy sorrow, sadness; hard to bear; an overcasting presence; dull and dim.

Healing is a process. It's just like doing a deep cleaning of the windows of your house—you don't just clean the outside. You have to remove the window's screen, use the proper cleanser to get into the deep crevices of the window's track and frame, spray it down, scrub it, and power wash. This is what the Lord desires to do for us, for our brokenness. He must go deep to clean the body, soul, and spirit.

Heaviness settled in me; bringing rejection, self-pity, a broken heart, insomnia, despair, loneliness, PTSD, dejection, deep inner hurt, hopelessness, depression, heaviness, suicidal thoughts, a grieving and torn spirit, sadness, sorrow, regret, and condemnation. It's a strongman, a head honcho, and it carries an intense and deliberate seduction of your mind and ultimately affects your physical body.

I read about a man who was diagnosed with depression at the age of fifteen. His doctor had prescribed a medication with severe side effects that threatened to push him deeper into depression and even suicide. He stated that even at his young age, he realized this drug was not the best choice. He continued to seek a cure for his depression and began to study the Bible, understanding that depression is directly addressed in the Word of God. He chose to use Isaiah 61:3 as an antidote, and was delivered by continually praising God and believing, just as the Scriptures indicate. What can we learn from this man? In his youth, he chose to seek God for his cure rather than a drug. Staying in God's Word and studying Scriptures specific to your situation will yield favorable results.

This spirit of heaviness had walked with me through most of my childhood and into my adult life, but solemnness became a daily part of my character. The physical burden I remember was daunting and will never be forgotten. To know that such a great stronghold of darkness could attach itself to me and reside comfortably in my being—even in the midst of cleansing—was bewildering to me. The intenseness and unrelenting determination of this spirit to destroy my mind provoked me to war against it. I knew its time was limited and that it intended to do as much damage as it could while it had a grip on me. When a spirit of heaviness enters your mind against your will, sets up residence there, and attempts to take control, it requires a deliberate battle through intentional and direct prayer to evict it. My experiences with rejection, separation, deep hurt, pain, death, divorce, suicidal thoughts, unforgiveness, betrayal, isolation, and physical and mental abuse were the catalyst for this strongman of heaviness to take residence in me during my childhood and spread evil roots that would linger with me into adulthood.

Wearing My Pain

My solemnness and depression were visible. I had insomnia, poor sleep patterns, severe weight loss and gain, a rollercoaster appetite, no interest or desire to do anything, flashes of anger, and a sense of being alone, rejected and isolated. I couldn't think. It was as if my thought process had slowed to a crawl; I couldn't concentrate. I couldn't cook—nothing. I lost the desire to do anything. It was as if my knuckles were dragging on the ground. Self-pity and low self-esteem became my daily bread, and I woke every morning with a dull, lifeless feeling. I could accomplish only the most routine and mundane tasks. I could feel the pressure in my mind.

When I was a teen, I was often asked, *"What's wrong? Why are you down? Why do you have a bad attitude with all that you have?"* Who knew? Who took the time to find out what was gripping me? Just recently, I came across my old identification cards from past years, and the pictures revealed to me the spirit of despair I wore on my face. At the time, I didn't see the heaviness that was upon me, but looking at these photos now, I gasped. The pictures depicted my state of entrapment.

Life Lesson: The Word of God speaks directly of this strongman, its characteristics, and God's predestined deliverance. Isaiah 61:3 states, "To appoint unto them that mourn in Zion, to give unto them beauty for ashes, the oil of joy for mourning, the garment of praise for the spirit of heaviness." I love this Scripture, for it proclaims that we already have the victory! The Lord tells us to appoint and to give. It's a gift, and it's ours. He lets us know clearly that He knows all about our state of mind and will bring us out of it. This was not a part of God's intended plan for us—it was not supposed to be that way. We must overcome this emotion, for it will cause excessive mourning and depression, a physical heaviness, sluggishness, tiredness, and a lack of drive and self-will. Its characteristics are so common that many people live day to day with it like it's a normal way of life. In this Scripture, God is specific as to what will break the bands and powers of darkness of this strongman. I did not feel victorious; I felt nothing but an oppressed state of mind. I struggled daily with a pursuit of happiness—beauty, joy, praise, strength, and righteousness. But in spite of what I felt, it was ultimately my weapon of praise that brought me victory in this battle of my emotions.

Time to Take Courage and Fight

As much as I thought on the Holy Scriptures—and at times, I didn't even have the mindset to hear a Scripture—this had become my daily conversation. I began to think about what my children would do without me. I had believed the lies of the enemy for so long that it was very hard to think positively. I was so weak, feeble-minded, and worn down. There were many long, dark nights that I cried. I pushed myself to sing spiritual songs of praise in my most painful moments, and I would always ask God if He heard me. Why did I have to I suffer like this, why divorce, why adultery, what did I do wrong?

Many times, there was not a sense of relief. I was in a routine that had no tangible positive results, but something in me just would not give up. But in my process, the Lord had to teach me that it takes discipline and obedience to serve and win in God. I had to learn to bring my will into God's will. It took commitment and an unshakeable discipline in all areas of my life to war in the spirit against this demonic oppression. God shows us the land and tells us that He has given it to us, just as he did to Joshua, but my hindrance was in the pursuit. As we see in Joshua 1:2, He told the children, "It's yours. I have given you rest." However, they had to strategically fight and rid the land of the inhabitants and subdue it—and it was the subduing where I failed miserably. I would simply pray and wait—with no action, no faith steps, nothing. I had no drive and no determination, and in my most miserable state when this strongman was racking my brain with thoughts of suicide, I just didn't get the fact that it would take an active, combative pursuit on my part. I had no idea that the Lord was making a warrior.

Resilience Will Win Battles

Determination, dedication, and discipline would become my key factors. I did not feel or have real hope of recovery from this divorce, and the words I spoke daily were seemingly empty, but God heard my words and read my heart. He promised in His Word to deliver, and all I knew was that He did not lie. The words of the enemy ravaged my mind with condemnation, self-pity, and regret. He would whisper to me, "Everyone hates you; you destroyed your family; God hates you; you will never recover; you will always be alone, and you are going to die lonely. Others are still married, so why would God do this to you?"

Shet up, devil! ~Pastor Renee Winston

These seemingly small statements from the devil are huge for someone suffering from depression and rejection. Had all of this really surfaced as a result of my divorce and his remarrying? It seemed like I was on the fast track to suicide.

Studies show that marital status' change represents a risk factor for suicidal behavior. The first year after the change is critical for elevated suicidal risk.

2006 to 2010 were four long years of suffering in divorce court. I was in a clinically depressed state, made life mistakes, and wasted time and money. These four years were the most malfunctioning years of my life. It was an all-out fight for my children and my mind. I was either going to fight and win, or die and lose the already victorious battle that Christ had secured on Calvary for me. My victory had already been won—I would no longer be bound by condemnation. There was no double jeopardy! The enemy always hits below the belt. He is relentless in his pursuit to take us out; so in turn, we must be even more determined to obtain every blessing given to us, including all the power against demonic spirits that the Lord has predestined for us.

Ephesians1:3 says, "Blessed be the God and Father of our Lord Jesus Christ, who hath blessed us with all spiritual blessings in heavenly places in Christ." Those spiritual blessings are what we must grab hold of and walk in. Luke 10:19 says, "Behold, I give unto you power to tread on serpents and scorpions, and over all the power of the enemy: and nothing shall by any means hurt you." We must truly believe in this. We must war with accurate, specific, and direct prayers to take out the enemy with boldness and without fear, with the knowledge and resolve that we will win. This strongman must be bound.

"No man can enter into a strong man's house, and spoil his goods, except he will first bind the strong man; and then he will spoil his house" (Mark 3:27).

Soul Strategy

We war as an infantry unit, a guided missile in prayer. There is no joint tenancy in our soul; the only one who should hold the deed is Jesus Christ. In my purification,

I asked the Lord by the pressing of the Holy Spirit to cleanse and purge me, to release me of what I could not put my finger on. As I grew spiritually, I began to realize something had a hold on me, because I kept reverting to those past tendencies and ways. I had to confront these tendencies and seek understanding to accurately and relentlessly combat this enemy. I had so much baggage and depressed thinking that needed to be unearthed and destroyed at the root. My thoughts were opening the door for the devil's oppression. My conscience was defeating me. I had to make an abrupt change and fight hard against the tactics and tools the enemy was using against my mind. The constant memory of my husband's infidelity and his blatant degrading of me, played like an old Gramophone with its distinct crackling in the background, skipping and repeating. Little by little, the Lord began to reveal the various spirits that bound my mind. The torment that comes with divorce is intolerable. I was determined to fight and began to search my inner self for what I felt in the Word of God. I found that in each and every emotion, I was the opposite of God's character, and so I hit it head-on and began to search for the truth. Only the Holy Spirit can reveal truth. The truth and how to rightfully apply it is what I needed to set me free.

"How be it when he, the Spirit of truth, is come, he will guide you into all truth: for he shall not speak of himself; but whatsoever he shall hear, that shall he speak: and he will show you things to come"
(John 16:13).

War Strategy

I met a former WWII Air Force Colonel who served General George S. Patton. He described a simple war strategy that painted a picture in my mind. He stated that he would fly General Patton over an area that they intended to bomb; identifying certain bridges and territories requiring elimination, which in turn, would keep the enemy from being able to flee or link up to reinforcements. I don't know about you, but this solidified for me the unavoidable task of watching as well as praying. Strategic prayer strategy and execution.

Just as the devil seeks those he can devour, we must be more aggressive and calculating while engaged in this war of our souls. I had to stand my ground and take back my authority. I spoke life and not death, and I praised God in spite of what I felt. My mind was not in a healthy place, but failure was not an option for me. I became intimately acquainted with the Word of God, and I attested only to victories in the middle of many battles. I learned to call on the name of the Lord, even without feeling. I didn't want to move on my emotions—I had done that all my life, and it hadn't worked. I had finally learned that God's way was foolproof. My prayer for freedom became a daily habit, and I practiced obedience without question. Most of the time, I didn't understand what God was doing, but I knew that my war with the enemy was already won.

It felt as if the more I prayed and obeyed the Lord, the more that spirit of heaviness squeezed me. One late afternoon in the Summer of 2012, I was walking through my home, and an overwhelming feeling of bewilderment hit me. I remember immediately stopping. I knew without a doubt it was the spirit of heaviness, and I had to acknowledge it to God. I screamed, "God, I am so tired! You have to deliver me! I can't go on like this! Help me!" I leaned on my living room wall and slid down to the floor. My tears began to flow, and through them, a surge of release came. The feeling of sadness left, and I felt a sense of confidence. By crying out to God with my whole heart, within seconds, I had just cast years of cares on Him.

"Lord, I cry unto thee: make hast unto me; give ear unto my voice, when I cry unto thee" (Psalm 141:1).

Being Pushed into the Unknown

I no longer held myself captive and I surrendered myself totally to the Lord. There was no more self-defense and no more protecting and fighting. I relinquished all my rights for retaliation and hate into the hands of the Lord. I wanted revenge for the pain the divorce caused, for my ex-husbands' irresponsibility to fidelity. It felt as if I had been unconsciously clenching my stomach muscles so tightly, and I suddenly released them. I went on with my day, and I had flutters of anticipation if something was going to happen. I didn't know what—I just knew something was going to happen. I had never felt a release like that before, and I began to attest. I truly turned it over to the Lord. The next morning when I woke for prayer, I felt strange and light. My very being no longer felt heavy like I had just stepped out of a pool and gravity was taking hold. I knew immediately I had been released! I began to touch my face, my arms, and my legs with giddiness. I said, "Oh my God! Oh my God; it's gone!" I had truly released it to Him after all these years, and He did just as only the Lord, strong and mighty, can do. He answered me. I dropped down to my knees and rejoiced in laughter and thankfulness. I was ecstatic! I had an overwhelming sense of praise and joy!

"Ask, and you will receive, that your joy may be full"
(John 16:24).

Journal Entry, 10/11/2012 – I see the Daughter of Zion, a woman of pristine character, full of prayer and compassion for souls to be set free, full of God's love. She is so pure. She is always in my visibility. I see her in my dreams.* God that is who you are making me to be— your *daughter. I will get there, day by day. I just want to be pure.

Indefatigable

Praise is a weapon that will never fail. I had to learn to obey the Scriptures without waiver and without question. The Word of God calls for us to *"Bless the Lord at all times; His PRAISE shall CONTINUALLY be in my mouth"* (Psalm 34:1, KJV). Whatever the emotional distress is, the level of blessing that God pours into you will exceed the attack. The very words that we speak are life or death, and these words alter the course of our life.

I began to realize that my words changed my thinking. I had started my own psychotherapy. I talked to myself and counteracted negative thoughts and ideas; simply everything the devil said. Was it perfect every time? No. Did

I have ups and downs? Yes. But I was not going to tire out or give up. It was a daily mind battle. As soon as I felt anything or thought anything opposite of the truth, I talked it through with the Word of God. I had to search the Scriptures to find me, to see what the Bible said about Angela and God; to find out who I was in Him and why He created me. I began to write and list every negative truth on one side of the page and find an opposing positive to list on the other side. I had to think right. My mindset mattered.

I had to realize that I didn't have to live in emotional misery from my divorce. No more regret of what my children's lives could have been like in a two-parent happy home. No more shame of the stigma of being a divorcee. I don't have to eat the crumbs as a dog from the table because I am divorced. I have a right to eat at the head of the table with the choicest meats. Who is society to blacklist me, and who am I to allow them to do so? — It was a lie from the devil. I had to learn that right thinking brought right results, and so I pressed and purposed my mind, heart, and soul, determined to grab onto this precious, blessed, highly honorable life that Jesus had died on the cross to give me. Why would I spoil it? Now that I had a grip on it, the spirit of heaviness would no longer operate in my life. I accepted God's grace, love, and freedom. I accepted life, and I would live and not die. As Christ is, so am I.

Truths:

1) Prayer strategy will always work.
2) It takes courage to make the hard adjustments in your life.
3) The determination to win is in your hands.
4) Internalizing and avoiding issues will cause distress.
5) Your level of blessing will exceed your attack.
6) Know that in life, there will be some setbacks, but there will also be many successes.
7) My marriage ended, not my life.

Notes: Write down what you are determined to change in your life, based on these truths.

1. _____

_____

2. _____

_____

3. _____

_____

4. _____

_____

5. _____

_____

6. _____

_____

Daily Affirmations: Speak daily with belief, passion, and energy. Digest each word until it becomes your truth.

1. I refuse to accept mediocrity.
2. I am committed to living an extraordinary life.
3. My mental state is what I make it. It's a mindset change.
4. The Lord considered me for this challenge, I accept.
5. My divorce was no surprise to God, He is using it for my GOOD!

CHAPTER FIVE: **BREAKING THE PAIN AND BITTERNESS**

"He heals the brokenhearted and binds up their wounds
[curing their pains and their sorrows]"
(Psalm 147:3AMP).

Pain = Acute mental or emotional distress or suffering

Root of Bitterness

Hebrews 12:15 (AMP) states, "Exercise foresight and be on the watch to look [after one another], to see that no one falls back from and fails to secure God's grace (His unmerited favor and spiritual blessing), in order that no root of resentment (rancor, bitterness, or hatred) shoots forth and causes trouble and bitter torment, and the many become contaminated and defiled by it."

Pain is a sensory reaction from the nervous system, which signals your mind that a part of your body is in danger. Emotions are an involuntary and normal response to pain. When our heart is feeling pain, the body almost cocoons. It's as if the body aches, and the pain is electrified and magnified. Emotional and physical pain can cause an increase in strength—it can make you better, or it can make you ugly, bitter, resentful, and weak. It can either make you or break you.

Pain, uncorrected, can allow bitterness to take root, and ultimately the pain that wreaked havoc daily in my mind made me bitter, resentful, and aloof. This pain was intense and sensory driven, and it convinced my mind that what I saw and thought were truth and death, but in reality, it was the devil's lies. The pain that blinded my mind was so intense; I thought that even after the situation was resolved, the pain would remain with me and linger as a part of my life. I made decisions, purchases, and plans for my immediate future based on this pain. The pain blinded the very functioning of my brain. I awoke morning after morning, fighting discouragement, and more times than I can remember, I threw in the towel. I wanted to quit trying so hard. Nothing in my life was looking like victory. The bitterness became cancerous; causing resentment and no hope of getting better. I thought all that I had ever done wrong in my life had now come raining down upon me. When emotional pain occurs, bitterness usually follows. The initial sting of the painful thing may be gone, but the bitterness can remain within.

The Bible describes what bitterness can do. Bitterness is defiling, quiet, and sneaky. A bitter person can radically corrupt anyone around them. Deuteronomy 29:18 describes it as a "root bearing poisonous fruit and wormwood." Bitterness can cause trouble, lead to unhealthy relationships and personal destruction. A bitter person can become as a serpent, spreading venom and laying cockatrice eggs.

"None calleth for justice, nor any pleadeth for truth: they trust in vanity, and speak lies; they conceive mischief and bring forth iniquity. They hatch cockatrice' eggs, and weave the spider's web: he that eateth of their eggs dieth, and that which is crushed breaketh out into a viper"
(Isaiah 59: 4-5).

A person bitter from pain is under the control of the spirit of bitterness. It wants to plant itself and spread. Its ultimate goal is to stay alive and spread to others through one's words.

Face It!

I had to face my bitterness when I thought that just saying, "I forgive" was enough. I had to realize bitterness is not an immediate, outward reaction, like fear or anger. Bitterness is subtle. If you don't recognize its traits, you will overlook this key hindrance to forgiveness. I began to notice a prevalent and uneasy feeling whenever I thought about past events, and when I talked about those past events, specifically my ex-husband the strange woman, and my step-father. I was brash and sharp with my opinion about them. My bitterness went undetected by me for quite some time. It began to be a daily struggle not to think about my divorce, my family, and my childhood. My bitterness grew and took on another face. I began to look different; I became disdainful and callous. Bitterness had taken root.

As a rule, roots of plants and trees grow beneath the surface. If they breach the surface, it's very evident—the leaves of the plant begin to turn brown. When this occurs, there is an immediate cause for concern. A palm tree planted too close to a home will search for water. Its roots will spread and wrap themselves around water pipes, choking the pipe and causing it to burst. Those roots can cause great damage that will require intense repair; thus, the bitterness of the soul. My pain, now transformed into bitterness, was not easy to deal with. But, I knew the source. The pain in my adulthood was caused by divorce, picturing my husband with another woman, his treatment of me, and the rejection of being cast off. My pain was the result of hearing my husband say, "I can't let her go. She means more to me than you, and I feel obligated to her. I just can't leave her."

Deal with the Root Cause

The pain was memories of my abusive childhood, the nightmares, the post-traumatic stress disorder, and the dysfunction it caused. The love and trust that I invested in my ex-husband which was refused was the agitating factor. I had tried so hard to run from that life, but I hadn't run far enough because it ended up right in my face as an adult with the demise of my marriage. How in the world did I get here? I thought the bitterness was over, but the demise of my marriage enabled it to rear its ugly head. It had remained hidden in previous years, awaiting the perfect time to strike and render me helpless and debilitated.

The thoughts of protecting my children from divorce, from mental and physical abuse, from detachment and separation—they started to seem dim and unattainable, a far-fetched idea only achievable by other families. My childhood memories rose up again, and the anger, pain, and bitterness infested me like never before. The devil was on an all-out assault on my mind. My ideas of marriage had never included a devastating end like this. The pain of not being given a chance to make what was wrong right made my days empty and fruitless. I blamed my ex-husband, and I blamed God. My anger and bitterness twisted my bowels. I began to hate and despise my ex-husband, other people, and life itself. I told God—and myself—that I had tried everything to be the best I could be, and it still hadn't worked. What else could I do? Why should I live? Bitterness would not allow me to see my fault and part in the marital distress.

I began to tell myself that I was the righteous one and I was the victim. I had done everything right and did not deserve to be rejected by my husband. This thought process brought a temporary peace, but I did not know that this too, was a trick of the enemy. I eventually fell into a "victim"

slump and concluded that I had wasted my time and my dream of having a loving and happy family was nonexistent.

Side Fact: *Not dealing with YOU is a predestined train wreck. Talking to yourself can be the most effective way to find out who you are, so have the courage, to be honest with yourself. Unrealistic conclusions will send you into depression based on a fantasy. Deal with yourself, and deal hard.*

Now let's go back to my state of mind in 2006. This was a year full of bitterness. A year when I fell deep into clinical depression—mood disorders, social isolation, paranoia, lack of sleep. I hid it from everyone. When I did sleep, I had nightmares. I was plagued by the riveting fear of leaving my children unprotected and alone. I was irritable and solemn. Bitterness began to grow as every thought of my marriage and my future was ripped out of my heart.

Identify Dysfunctional Living

I went to church depressed and left a little happier, but there was no joy and no real hope in my mind. I couldn't believe that it wasn't all a bad dream. When nightfall came, depression was knocking at my door. I let him in, and he stayed. No one really knew the nights of torment I endured when the enemy consumed me. It was a takeover attempting my mind, and all was working against me. My children were distressed and began wetting their beds and having angry and fearful outbursts. I learned that this is what happens to a family when the covering is removed. What most men don't know is that when they remove themselves from the covenant of marriage and the home, it's a free-for-all for the enemy to launch a ravenous attack on the wife and children. Husbands protect their families spiritually whether they live for the Lord or not because marriage is a spiritual covenant, and the enemy recognizes the man as the head.

It was as if I was standing in the middle of a deep forest with my children nestled in a small cave directly behind me. I had to fight off the wolves that attacked from all sides. These wolves symbolized the spirits attempting to get to my children and me, to disrupt and disfigure our destiny. I struggled with unbelief and the lack of faith, but I fought with all I had. The wolves of anger, depression, poverty, fear, loneliness, suicide, and rejection often bombarded me. I fought and fought, and I prayed. I walked my small apartment's living room floor, crying out to God to HELP ME and cover my children. Only He knew what was going on and why. I learned how to function in a dysfunctional state of mind. Little by little, I rested in the resolve that all things happen for a reason, but I didn't know the reason, and that was my agony.

Dysfunctional and Bitter

I struggled to leave my home. I calculated daily the directions to my job. It took mental effort and strength. My depression and bitterness caused me to shut down and not socialize. The most I engaged in at work was a brief hello and goodbye to coworkers. I ate lunch alone, worked alone, wore headphones, and didn't want to be bothered. Most of the mental strength was used up in fighting my ex-husband's lawyer's attacks and attempts to separate me even more from my children. The more time he had on the books, the less money he'd have to pay—and that was his greatest concern. I was determined not to allow my children's lives to be dictated by child support. My bitterness grew. I loathed people; married men were appalling to me, and the very thought of marriage made me angry and sick.

My hair began to shed and recede. Bitterness was making me look as ugly as I felt. I began to ask myself why I hadn't known about this side of marriage. Who was there to help me? Why was I so alone in this? Why was this happening to me? *I didn't realize that this pain had a perfect purpose and would be used to perfect my purpose.*

I struggled daily with life. My self-esteem was beyond destroyed, and I had no idea how to put the little bitty pieces of my life that were left back together. I didn't have any self-esteem before the adultery and divorce, which made all that I ever thought about me become my reality. Suicidal thoughts set in, and when my children would leave to be with their father, those feelings were prevalent. I would hear a voice in my head saying, "What do you have to live for? It doesn't matter whether you live or not; no one cares. You can never fix this for your children. You have no purpose in life. There is nothing left for you." I remember these words so clearly. I listened and pondered on each statement the devil made to me, and I struggled to shut him off, but could not. I would go for long drives, and while driving, the devil would tell me to drive off the road or an embankment, to hit a tree and end my life. I was hiding inside of myself, hiding from life and suicide. I survived night after night in a deep, dark place until sunrise, and then I would get up, put my "mommy hat" on, and try to make my children's lives as normal as possible.

On an Ugly Edge

Bitterness consumed my mind and body. It affected my weight, my organs, and, of course, my mood. I was snappy and lacked patience. Everything my children did irritate me—every sound, every cry, and even laughter. My heart palpitated, and I took deep breaths to ease my anxiety. When I felt as if I would go over the edge, I would remove myself from the presence of my children because I did not want to yell at them and hurt them because of my own irritation. I would catch myself yelling when I did not mean to, and then I'd cry because I didn't know how to handle the pressure of maintaining my finances, housing, and employment in addition to giving my children the extra attention they needed because their father was no longer there.

In August of 2006, we moved into a small low-income apartment. The kids thought it was fun at first, but then they began to be fearful of every sound and every creak. I was afraid, too. I was spooked and my nerves were on edge most of the time. We were scared at night, and I would sit up most of the night, afraid and crying and lonely. I knew I had to get some sleep—my depression and bitterness was pulling at my mental state in an awful and deteriorating way. My son said to me one night, "Mommy, I'm scared. Can't we put the chair under the door handle?" So, I placed my sofa chair under the door handle to keep it from being turned, and this gave me some solitude.

Days came and went, and we tried to adjust. The children had a tough time adjusting to the time split between mommy and daddy, and it cut me to the core. My baby boy who was four years old at the time began to wet the bed. My seven-year-old began to lash out in angry outbursts, asking for his father and asking why he had left and why he wasn't there. He became defiant and often hit the walls and slammed doors, screaming, "You made my daddy go away!" Where was he getting this behavior from? I became angry thinking about what my children were being told when they left home with their father. My son was so hurt and bitter at such an early age. I thought, "He shouldn't be feeling this way. His father should be here to answer his questions. His father should be the one feeling what I am feeling." My baby was bitter, and my mind was slipping away.

I began to work on my son daily. I talked with LJ, refusing to let his outburst move me or cause me to resent him. He was bitter, and I had to help LJ, or it would overtake him as it had overtaken me. I prayed and pleaded for his soul. I worked on his behavior and channeled his anger. I gritted my teeth and tried not to let his angry words affect me. He even began to grow angry with his dad. His little emotions were so torn and confused. This went on for four years.

But what I realized was that just as I was molding and reshaping his mind away from bitterness, I could get the same results in myself. I had slipped into a suicidal state, often asking myself what I had to live for. My life was a wreck. It always had been, but I had never addressed it. It wasn't that my ex-husband had left me for another woman or the unanswered questions about my childhood abuse—the devil had me convinced that God was against me and that He did not love me. My emotional pain had gone beyond the things of man and had everything to do with God. It felt like multiple personalities were taking over my mind, and I didn't know who I was.

Bitterness has multiple connectors that all work in sequence. Bitterness can't be present without anger, and anger can't be present without hurt. Neither can hurt be present without rejection and fear.

The depression I dealt with was painful, and my mind was not created to support this type of devastation, confusion, and pain without a defense—and I had none. I struggled to keep a sound mind. I cried more than I had ever cried in my life. I cried while brushing my teeth while combing or washing my hair, while driving in the car, and while shopping in the store. I cried all the time because I was dying inside. I know now that it was the death of all the toxic feelings, and that crying was washing and cleansing me. But at the time, I didn't know it was a good death and a releasing of my pain. I have come to understand that the pain the devil had meant to use for evil, God had intentionally orchestrated into purpose.

"And we know that all things work together for good to them that love God, to them who are the called according to his purpose" (Romans 8:28 NLT).

I struggled with friendships and associations. I was estranged from my family and tore myself away from everyone as much as I could. My best friend was right there for me, dealing with my ups and downs. She cried with me and gave me words of encouragement and her shoulder to lean on. But it seemed as if no one could penetrate my mind or heart. My bitterness caused idleness and lonely days and gave me plenty of time for unhealthy thoughts. Spiritually, I was depleted. I took my physical body to church when I could, but my spirit was at home, hiding and waiting to be rescued. I was lifeless and discombobulated, and the thought of living brought on immense fear. My body began to feel the effects of my unhealthy thinking. You see, our minds set the stage for success or failure, and my mind had been tricked by the enemy. There was no doubt the devil's attack on my life was a direct hit. Divorce is a tsunami and your emotions are the aftermath.

"Be well balanced (temperate, sober of mind), be vigilant and cautious at all times; for that enemy of yours, the

devil, roams around like a lion roaring [in fierce hunger],
seeking someone to seize upon and devour"
(1 Peter 5:8 AMP).

It is imperative that we use the Word of God as a weapon. God knows exactly what's going on. With Him, nothing occurs by chance, and nothing is a shock. Every situation has an intended purpose. Although nothing in my conscious mind thought spiritually at all, my subconscious mind held God's hand.

The bitterness gripped me for four long, depleting years. So much wrong was happening that I gave up. My heart stopped hoping, and this was a major mistake because hope was all I had.

Yet, in these four years, the Lord never let me go. He continued to tear down, feed, rebuild and restock my soul. He told me, *"This is the making of you."* The Lord told me I was bitter, but I didn't know how to give my bitterness to Him. I knew His voice, but I did not believe that my life would change. The devil had convinced me that this was the way it would be until I died; that it was repayment for past sin.

But the devil is a liar! Romans 8:1 states, "Therefore (there is) now no condemnation (no adjudging guilty of wrong) for those who are in Christ Jesus, who live [and] walk not after the dictates of the flesh, but after the dictates of the Spirit." The devil will use your past and twist it as if you are not forgiven. He will cause you to take the bitter bait and believe his lies, and the result will be depression, lack of hope, and bitterness. "Not a novice, lest being lifted up with pride he fall into the condemnation of the devil" (1 Timothy 3:6).

Wow! God knows what He is talking about. I had to get into the Word of God and study my way out of bitterness. I began to fight. I know I talk about fighting in my mind a lot, but that is because the protection and control of your mind is critical to your success.

I was in a Sunday morning service one week, desperately wanting my life to change. The Lord said to me, "No more, Mara!" (Ruth 1:20). I had been bitter for so long that it had become a crutch in my life. I had to learn that my mindset was what controlled my destiny—be it twenty minutes or twenty years from now. My perspective on life, success, rebuilding, and even failure was all controlled by my mind. If our minds can be transformed and changed to do evil, they can also be transformed and changed to do what is good—it's the same process, the same mind. I began to listen to the small, still, voice that said, *"Keep your eyes on me."* I had nothing to lose, but everything to gain.

Side Fact: *You will begin to see that your pain is not taking away from you, it's adding to you. It takes power and tenacity to change and move forward after divorce or abuse. Toughness is a gift. Begin to see adversity as a step toward a greater you. What is painful also has so much purpose.*

As I studied the Scriptures, I became driven by the Word of God that dealt with the mind. I had to realize that in the most desperately bitter and disgruntled time in my life, it was going to take a change of mind. Then and only then, did I begin to find peace and soundness of mind. We feel what we are thinking, and it's not a feeling at first but only a thought. I had to fully maximize the use of my brain, telling it what to create, and this was a daily challenge. But because I had the power to create my own atmosphere, the sky was the limit. If I asked myself a question and wasn't specific on my intended outcome, I could spend all day thinking, creating things, and guessing but never truly achieving my desired result. However, when I began to tell my brain, "This is what you will think, this is what we will do, don't think that, or throw that out because it's evil and not good"—only then did my pain cease. Wow!

"As a man thinketh in his heart, so is he"
(Proverbs 23:7).

The mind is capable of thinking good and evil. Evil can take over and control your thinking as it did mine. *I had to learn that my character is a summary of all of my thoughts.* I was bitter, and that bitterness took deep root in my soul and branched out like a fertile mulberry tree.

I had to learn the art of restful alertness. I had to learn the true meaning of patience, of waiting worry-free without anxiety or a feeling of hurriedness, of having confidence and joy in the process. I needed *"strength to endure until the promise came."* I had to be alert and diligent in my emotions and feelings, determined daily to see change and the annihilation of the enemy's residue in my soul. It was as if I was at war. Part of me was on the wall with night vision goggles, and another part of me was enjoying my children as I laughed, rejoiced, and praised God for the impending victory. I had to decide to misuse my brain no longer. I had to decide not to waste the precious and overabundant life that the Lord gave me.

I had a choice, and so I began to change the way I thought. Instead of thinking of each day as a day of misery, I began to think of each day as a day of opportunity. How could I change me today? What could I master and accomplish today? Even if nothing changed, I held on to hope and to the fact that it *would* change. I began to realize that if I remained bitter and angry, neither my children nor I would be able to benefit from a healthy and sane life. My everyday thoughts became the promises of God, and my life began to have purpose based on my thoughts. I had no idea that my pain and struggle was purposeful, but there was something in me that—no matter how I felt or how suicidal the thoughts that flooded my mind—would not let me quit. I knew my answer lay in Jesus. I had to get closer to Him; I could not let the enemy win.

I now knew that I would be safe in the arms of the Lord. I chose to heal, no matter what it took. I didn't know how long it would take, but God promised me in His Word that He would never leave me nor forsake me, and that is what I held onto.

I had to allow God to heal all my pain. First, I acknowledged the pain and the dysfunction. Then I asked God to heal me and allowed God to do it no matter how hard it got. I was specific in my pursuit. I realized that my life could have been much worse; I was alive and not dead. The Lord told me to praise Him and to give Him thanks in spite of my circumstances. He reminded me of the Scripture. No matter what happened, I forced myself to say, "Thank You, Lord," and my daily plea to God was "I trust you."

You don't need the person who hurt you to survive, but you do need God to live.

Of course, my new resolve of faith was challenged, so even when I lost in family court, I said, "Thank you, Lord" with tears in my eyes. On the days that were full of pain, ridicule, and despair, I said, "Thank you, Lord." I did not give up. There were many tests, but I praised God and spoke His Word, not by emotions, but out of obedience. My praise became my weapon and prayer was my daily launching ground. I cried out to the Lord, "Oh Lord, heal me, help me; reveal this ugly heart!" I was in bewildering despair, but something in me would not accept the way I felt—I could not give up hope of my healing. And God began to walk with me every step of the way. I turned my emotional issues over to God. *My healing came with pain and a purpose.* The pain was finding out how truly ugly, worn, torn, captured, and emotionally distressed I was. In childbirth, the labor pains and the pains of the actual birth have a purpose. The purpose is the miracle being brought forth. I chose to see myself healed, and I looked at this healed woman daily. She seemed but a stone's throw away. She was just that close. I smiled at her, and she smiled back at me. And then I knew this pain was going to be short-lived.

Truths:

1) Bitterness will destroy you, not your ex.
2) Only God can heal your brokenness.
3) You build your self-image with your own thoughts.
4) It hurt; it wasn't fair; you want revenge.

Notes: Write down what you are determined to change in your life, based on these truths.

1. _____
   _____
2. _____
   _____
3. _____
   _____
4. _____
   _____
5. _____
   _____
6. _____
   _____

Daily Affirmations: Speak daily with belief, passion, and energy. Digest each word until it becomes your truth.

1. There is greatness inside of me.
2. Jesus' plan of redemption was created just for me.
3. I accept myself, I love myself
4. I matter, and I am loved.

CHAPTER 6:

THE POWER OF FORGIVENESS

Where there is forgiveness there is freedom; your
actions must support your emotions.
~Angela D. Holmes

Am I not destroying my enemies when I make friends
of them? ~Abraham Lincoln

Forgiveness Is Supernatural

God is interested in changing you more than He is interested in changing your offender or your situation. So, let's start by asking God to change you first. There are some needful things in life, and forgiveness is one of them. We will be offended many times in our life, and lack of forgiveness will spiral us into a dark, dismal place of sickness and bitterness.

Unforgiveness is a bitter, cancerous worm that eats into the depths of your emotions. One of the hardest things in life to do is to forgive someone very close to you who deeply hurt you. Unforgiveness spreads like a wild cactus, pricking everyone in its reach and hurting anyone who tries to get close to you.

Forgiveness causes change, and change is seldom welcomed. It takes faith to forgive. Forgiveness is not negotiating repentance, and it's not a bargaining tool used to trap the offender. Forgiveness is a conscious choice made by your free will. It is a critical challenge for many of us. It's certainly not easy, but it is absolutely necessary. Let's define forgiveness. It is your decision to release all anger, malice, resentment, and feelings of being "owed." It is a choice you make to let all of these things go. Forgiveness is not a feeling but a choice, a choice to obey regardless of your feelings until it becomes a part of your heart. Forgiveness is something your offender can't tolerate, but it will liberate you. When you forgive, you are free to love. Forgiveness is a commandment and an essential part of your life. Forgiveness does not take away the responsibility of the offender to make their wrong right (although that may never happen). It does not belittle or minimize your pain. But it does mean that you choose not to retaliate or hold resentment. It frees you as the victim and allows you to take your power back from the offender. You decide not to be held hostage.

Forgiveness is a kingdom key. Our forgiveness rides on our ability to forgive others. It is a solidifying stake, a guaranteed release from the imprisonment of your mind. Forgiveness is strength. Only a strong, mature, and whole person can forgive. Forgiveness frees God to recompense you for the wrong forced upon you. When we hold unforgiveness, God's hands are tied, and He cannot fight for you.

Studies show that our past experiences govern our level of forgiveness.

Past experiences often determine how people will handle the same situation in the future. Forgiveness is a learned behavior. What we've experienced in the past and what we've been taught determines how we will react or respond. As I studied the resistance to and the importance of forgiving, the research indicated that our exposure to forgiveness—or lack of it—molds our choices later in life. According to Changingminds.org there are three periods of value development—Imprint, Modeling, and Socialization.

Let's focus on the Imprint period. From birth to seven years of age, our learned experiences are formed when we mimic what we see. We develop actions as a result of what is said to us and what we observe.

We adopt our parents' beliefs and choices as valid and true. This critical stage was the most damaging for me as it is for most of us. Remember our lineage, our inherited weaknesses, and our passed-down traits? This all factor in our healing. Did we watch our family members fight? Did we hold resentment and anger? I was stuck in that place for years—my stepfather was no longer alive, but I still carried bitterness, unforgiveness, hate, and shame long after he passed away. I had to make the choice to deal with my emotions concerning my stepfather. I had to choose to allow the Lord to show me where I was stuck, and I had to bring it to reality in my mind by verbalizing the truth about how I felt. The Lord led me back to where I had left off in this matter, and He made me a way for me to deal forcefully with it so that I could be free. Forgiveness, or lack thereof, can be bound in a family, and until we break this chain of bondage, we cannot be set free. You see, the devil thinks he has rights to the areas of your life that you don't deal with—he sees it as unprotected ground and will move in at any cost.

So, we must guard our thoughts because that is how he is going to keep the tape playing. He starts in the mind, but we must remember that our mind is a vast, powerful tool that we can use to fight the good fight of faith! When you forgive, you remove your judgment on the offender. Your heart turns to compassion, mercy, generosity, and concern; replacing resentment, bitterness, and distance.

When you hold on to past hurts, you're pushing the "go" button for failure.

What Are You Thinking?

We must change the way we think. We choose our thought patterns based on the information before us. We make decisions to think and act either negatively or positively. We must fight against the impure, unprofitable, and dead thoughts that surface daily. Our thoughts should produce life, bring a sense of happiness and resolution, and prosper us. We can change our life and our destiny if we change our thinking. Every thought we have reinforces or establishes a belief about something. Ask yourself some questions. What have I learned about forgiveness? What are the benefits of forgiveness? Are you withholding the pain? Then, digest your answers.

"Summing it all up, friends, I'd say you'll do best by filling your minds and meditating on things true, noble, reputable, authentic, compelling, gracious—the best,

not the worst; the beautiful, not the ugly; things to praise, not things to curse" (Philippians 4:8, MSG).

Forgiveness must be from the heart. There is a process of true forgiveness. First, repent to God and acknowledge your lack of forgiveness for your offender. Second, shut that door, so this step in the process is secure. Third, give unforgiveness no room to operate. The root of bitterness and unforgiveness must be destroyed. It must be bound, and the spirit of peace, joy, love, and a sound mind let loose. Many people rely on the fact that they "feel" better. If the offender apologized, they say, "Oh, I'm done with that" or "I've moved on." But if the root is not destroyed, it will arise again in your actions and attitudes toward everyday life and your new and current relationships. It will reveal itself in harsh and abrupt words related to the situation you were in, or in a severe dislike of marriage if you have been divorced. You will make negative remarks about men and maybe not want others to marry. You might even move onto another relationship but have trust issues or a fear of physical or verbal abuse. All of these bitter and negative reactions and comments result from the pain that you never admitted, the pain you hid from. You never dug up the real root or allowed the Lord to destroy it. These are true signs of unforgiveness.

Deal and Deal Hard

Often times, God is using the very thing you are praying against to make you who He wants you to be. So, deal precisely with the issue at hand, confront your issues, and don't place them on a shelf and ignore them. Acknowledge your pain, and recognize the resentment, anger, bitterness, and hate. Accept the part you played. You cannot afford not to forgive! Restoration will only come when you expose and destroy the root of the issue. Fight the fear of reliving the moment—it will pass. Indeed, it is the work of the enemy to steer you away from emotional freedom and keep your mind in a dismal state. Deal and deal hard.

Forgiveness is an act of the will, and the will can function regardless of the temperature of the heart.
~Corrie ten Boom

God Tells You How

You trap yourself and hold back the hand of the Lord's judgment when you don't forgive. Forgiving your ex-husband takes understanding. The Scriptures were written as a blueprint for every situation in our lives. As I began to recognize the hand of the Lord in my life and the fact that it was not an option for me to stay in unforgiveness because of how the Lord was preparing me to impact the lives of His people, I asked God, "How do I forgive, and why is it so hard to do so?" This Scripture immediately played in my mind: *"For all have sinned and come short of the glory of God"* (Romans 3:23). This was a moment of epiphany for me. Why are they unforgivable, but you are forgivable?

This is Hard, God!

Let me relay some of my struggles to you and tell you how God helped me to overcome them. I just could not wrap my mind around what was required of me. I stalled my process because I did not deal with the pain and did not address what was real and I pushed through it, gritting my teeth and smiling. I was a wreck inside because I could not understand the process of my healing. I had to go through the process of forgiveness, but I did not want to accept that. I wanted my heart whole, but I did not want to forgive. It was like trying to clean up a one hundred car train wreck with my bare hands.

I knew I had to go hard to change myself. Becoming free became a mainstay in my life. I gave over my will continually but did not see results right away. Was it easy? No, not at all. Each time I met my enemies or those I felt had wronged me; I would ask the Lord, "How did I do? Are you pleased? Did I do it from my heart?" As I began to see and understand what the Lord was asking of me as His daughter, it became a deliberate and purposeful action. I wanted only to yield the blessed results of a free and loving heart. Honestly, it hurt, and I had to face the fact that those I thought had truly loved me actually did not, and this was like a wrecking ball to my soul.

I loathed my ex-husband and had thoughts of his demise. My reasoning was that I had done nothing to deserve what I felt were heinous acts against me. How could I "love" only those who treated me well? My ex-husband James has a weakness, a limp that I don't have. Would I consider infidelity and act upon it? No, but James did, he lived a secret life. Could it possibly be that he recognized his errors but fell victim to pride? Do I breeze over the scripture that says, "Blessed are the merciful: for they shall obtain mercy" (Matthew 5:7)? I had to deal with what was real—I had to hit every hindrance in my life head-on with direct and deliberate reality checks and prayer. I had to ask myself the tough questions and listen to the tough answers. I came to the realization that a person can only hurt what they don't love, what they have no regard for. So, I asked myself, "Who have you hurt?" I had to ask and answer some serious questions. "Love never fails, so quite possibly, Angela, it was never love." I accepted the fact that based on the Word of God; it was not love. So, with that resolve, I stopped fighting the healing process.

My feelings and actions before I surrendered had been based on what I was thinking carnally. But the Lord allowed me to understand spiritually. He avenged me, so I didn't have to fight to prove to my enemy that they had not defeated me. God promised to do that for me. What more could I ask for? The Master Builder Himself was creating a vessel fit for the master's use. Forgiveness is a kingdom key!

When love hurts, love until it doesn't hurt anymore.
~Andrew Hart, The Victory Room

Stay the Course — No Quitters Here

My course was orchestrated by the Lord. Whatever my enemies asked for or did was not of their own free will, but somehow, they were used to execute situations in my life because it was the plan of God all along to heal and make me whole. "Forgive and live" became my mantra. When the dust settled, and I became more spiritually connected to God, then came the time for complete deep healing of my soul; that inward part that is nestled deep in the subconscious mind, deep in the dark ugly of my heart. So, I began to pinpoint Scriptures and material that dealt with forgiveness. I began to work on me. It was draining, and hard because I struggled to let go of what I knew to be my truth. The truth was what existed, was different from what I had thought and learned as a child. But because I'd lived with a false reality of myself, it was what I had established as my belief and truth. I had told myself that I was not good enough to be loved based on past experiences. My emotions and life had followed suit.

My ex-husband was never kind, and he didn't even acknowledge me with a simple wave or hello. He did this in front of our children, and it made me furious, especially when my children would ask, "Mom, why won't Dad talk to you?" The phone calls and texts were disrespectful and arrogant. But I had to hold my peace, as the Lord did not allow me to retaliate. The Lord said to me, "Be without reproach." So, I cried unto the Lord and asked, "Why are you allowing James to treat me this way when I've done nothing wrong?" The Lord quickly reminded me of this Scripture, "And we know that all things work together for good to them that love God, to them who are the called according to His purpose" (Romans 8:28).

God will not ask us to do something that He has not already given us the victory over. We are lacking absolutely nothing in Christ Jesus. I realized that I did not have to earn His grace—He gave it to me freely. I did not deserve it, and it was nothing I earned. His grace empowered and equipped me for the battle. I had to accept and realize that God was after me. He was preparing me for His great army of strong spiritual warriors. Luke 6:28 has specific instructions. We are to love, bless, do well, and pray for our offender. We are to give moral kindness to the offender and have compassion for them and care for them as a soul in need. This may seem far-fetched depending on where you are in the process, but it is your ultimate reality, just as it became mine. We must go beyond the offense with the tools that the Lord has given us. He knew that there would be offenses, and He also knew that the devil would try and use these offenses to distance you from Him. So, God gave foolproof Kingdom keys, and one of them is forgiveness. It will totally cleanse, heal, and set you free. In the midst of the pain, things are not easy, but if you set your heart and mind to it, it's more than obtainable. I had to realize that.

There were innumerable times when I did what the Scripture asked of me through obedience until it became a part of my heart. I wanted to please the Lord in every way that He required. It took persistence, determination, and a commitment to myself, but it was a part of the process of creating the new me. With each step forward, I had to be confident that it was going to work.

To be unforgiving is like to drink poison and wait for someone else to die! ~Bishop T. D. Jakes

Forgive? But How?

Do well and forgive—even when it hurts so badly! I am sure you are saying, "That's easier said than done. I just can't forgive like that. It's too hard." Well, I can relate. I went from gritting my teeth to verbalizing my desires, to immediately reaching out to the Lord in prayer because the breaking and remolding of me was painful. I continued steadfastly, although unwillingly at first and murmuring and complaining. I was physically sick from believing the lies the enemy told me, sick from believing that my forgiveness had allowed my enemies to "get away" with what they had done. When I realized that my forgiveness was changing my physical appearance, I regressed and became fearful of failure. I did not think I was going to make it mentally. Become ugly or forgive? It was hard for me because unforgiveness had been embedded in me from my family. I had family members who held unforgiveness for years— some were dead, but some were alive but not in their right mind. I thought to myself, *"How am I going to overcome this?"* I began to think about the life I had already lost. My days were passing me by, and nothing would change until I did. Deciding not to take the wrongs of others personally was hard because I wanted revenge. I wanted them to hurt as I did. Nevertheless, I created a plan to move from a lack of forgiveness to a life filled with joy and forgiveness. I would like to share with you a few steps you can take to deal with your difficulty to forgive:

1) Decide to deal with what's real. I had to make a conscious decision and talk to myself and deal with a real reality, not the false one that I had bought into. I made a decision to no longer agree with what rejection, belittlement, hate, abandonment, and betrayal said to me.

2) Journal and talk to God. I can't emphasize this enough. Write in your journal daily. Talk to God. Be honest with your feelings. Your journaling is between you and God. Once I realized this, I cried as

I wrote my thoughts. Writing will allow you to release your pain and get it out of your head. Write down the act and the emotions connected with it. Get it out of you and onto paper.

3) Pray without ceasing and be persistent. Set a prayer schedule for yourself. Bring God your thanksgiving and praise tell God all that concerns you. Do this throughout the day to keep your mind balanced. Be focused and be relentless. With regular prayer intervals, you are preventing yourself from falling into depression and bitterness. The ups and downs you may experience in your day won't affect you if you take it to your Father and release it.

4) Check yourself. Don't overlook your emotions! Deal with them, and deal hard. It's not just the way you are. Play the hand that you have been dealt. Play to win, and plan to destroy every cancerous emotion that resides in you. Be focused on healing and getting your emotions under control.

Journaling was the beginning of my release. I wrote descriptively about the pain and the offense. I thought about my ex-husband, the strange woman and my deceased stepfather (oh did I say he was deceased?) See throughout these writings you hear me refer to him, the pain he caused, and my emotions about him was just as heightened as with my ex-husband. But he's dead and has been since 1997! I allowed the painful memory of him to still be alive in my heart. Wow girly! Now how did the enemy get in? Who can stand against the wiles of the devil if they don't have a spiritual defense? How can one choose to live, do, and think differently without the power of God? "Forgive and be blessed, Angela" is what I told myself. This was my wake-up call, my door-shutting moment. I was now on the offensive side. Am I going to choose life or death? I began to release myself to the process, exactly as the Lord intended it to be. God's promises for my life became clear and present. I wanted so badly to live the life that the Lord had so eloquently created and designated for me. I was exuberant and overjoyed at the thought of being free. I had to think and speak my healing and deliverance daily. I began to visualize and study God's promises for His children. I had a lot of mirror moments and did a lot of self-talk, saying to myself, *"Now wait a minute, Angela; this life that has been entrusted to you is a magnificent gift from God. He has a purpose and plan that He is unfolding right before your eyes. You have to let go of the world, Angela. Let go of the shame and the betrayal. Let go of the anger, the hate, and the fear of starting over. Hold your head up high, square your shoulders, and live!"*

I had to be willing to accept that this suffering was a part of building me up to a place of strength and tenacity. Yes, this broken heart was a part of the plan. I went through making bad decisions, being lied on, ridiculed, and laughed at. I went through child custody battles, my home in foreclosure, hunger and unemployment. I was the last laugh for my ex-husband. But God's Word comes alive and is lived through us. We can get through life's events. I had to get there—it was my place of refuge. Truth be told, God chose me; I did not choose myself.

Forgiveness Starts in the Mind

I can't stress this enough. If your mind does not change, you will not change. The lack of forgiveness should be resolved as a "clear and present danger." The battle to forgive is not physical; it is spiritual, and it starts in the mind. It takes an intentional effort to fight the thoughts and temptations of the mind. The thought must be brought into captivity, under your control. You hear the thought, and you have the power to stop it from being planted. Just speak the Word of God against it. What did God say? You have to learn your enemy, learn the thoughts and feelings that the enemy uses to tempt you. Self-talk and more self-talk—and oh, did I mention self-talk?

When you truly forgive, you choose not to remember the offense, the pain, and destruction; just as the Lord remembers our sins no more.

"I, even I, am he that blotted out thy transgressions for mine own sake, and will not remember thy sins"
(Isaiah 43:25).

We can truly forgive and allow ourselves to be healed just as He has done. I surrendered and told the Lord that this was what I wanted. Just as you are, so am I. Give me this tool that you use. I saw the liberty in it, and it had been right under my nose the entire time. "Father, You said it is Your good pleasure to give us the keys of the Kingdom." Keys open things—greater revelation on issues, passageways, gifts, and abilities can come from the opening of something, and we want and need access to the Kingdom, the knowledge, authority, and power. We must bind up what is not expedient, and that is what will free us. So why does God choose not to remember our sins? Our sins would continually be before Him as the wicked is, and as long as sin is before God, his anger is kindled. As long as we remember the sin of our offender, the anguish and pain will cause a stumbling block in our lives. We will not be able to live as the Lord intended for us to live. He knows what the remembrance of sin does to our mind and the choices we will make because of it. We don't have the mental capacity to handle it—our revenge will be temporal, and short-lived. We must release the offender through forgiveness and allow the Lord to avenge us of our adversary.

We must trust God's Word in order to obey His Word. We have to trust that what He says the benefit will be and trust His instructions to forgive. If we are confident of God to avenge us, our souls are then freed from the tormentor, from the bondage, and from the strongman of heaviness. If we trust God to heal us, we then can release it into His hands and His judgment and rest in the security that we know without a doubt that He is for us, because He is righteousness. The releasing of your natural offender will bring you justice, and God loves justice.

With that said, I relinquished my desire for fleshly revenge (tit for tat). Unforgiveness is a wicked slow-cooking destroyer. It's a cankerworm, eating and twisting the soul from one place to another. Every aspect of our lives is driven by the bitterness, hate, score, and reproach. It chokes the very life out of you, causing anxiety, stress, ulcers, and hair loss. It will cause you to have unhealthy relationships with your children, your coworkers, your friends, and even your future mate. It will hinder your destiny and shipwreck the most important parts of your life.

God cares about our pain, our anxieties, and our concerns. In His timing and His way, offenses will be put before the Lord to judge. So, resist the temptation to avenge. Remember what the Lord promises in this powerful Scripture, Psalm 23:5, *"Thou prepares a table before me in the PRESENCE of mine enemies."* He spoke to my spirit, and He was talking to all that the enemy had done. He spoke to the verbal and physical abuse, wantonness, hate, forgiveness, bitterness, heaviness, oppression, lack of self- worth, fear, betrayal, rejection. He spoke to the little girl trapped inside of me. He knew all the devil had done and all that this flesh loved. It was time to be avenged, to take this situation and build from it; to allow a new direction in my life to be revealed.

Whatever you suppressed or were unable to get healing or closure on will not just disappear. It must be confessed, dealt with, and destroyed. My loneliness and the effects of a dysfunctional childhood were the catalysts for a victorious cleansing of my soul and the destruction of my pain. I was considered. I am a daughter of the King, a

Daughter of Zion. I would not give back a tear for what the Lord has done so beautifully in my heart.

"And thou, O tower of the flock, the strong hold of the Daughter of Zion, unto thee shall it come, even the first dominion; the kingdom shall come to the daughter of Jerusalem" (Micah 4:8).

Truths:

1) When I don't remember the offense, my anger won't be kindled.
2) Forgive quickly, minimize hurt, and always maximize forgiveness.
3) Forgiveness is not an option; it's a commandment.
4) Forgiveness is a Kingdom Key.
5) No other option but to deal with what's real.
6) Will it be easy? No! Beneficial? Yes!

Questions for you to ponder, actions for you to take:

1) What mindset shift are you going to make in your healing process?
2) Do you have the courage to forgive?
3) Are you ready to live a happy, healed life?

4) List the people you need to forgive and ask yourself why you haven't forgiven them. Confess how you have treated them for the way they treated you and destroy it.

Notes: Write down what you are determined to change in your life, based on these truths.

1. _____

_____

2. _____

_____

3. _____

_____

4. _____

_____

5. _____

_____

6. _____

_____

Daily Affirmations: Speak daily with belief, passion, and energy. Digest each word until it becomes your truth.

1. I will no longer be handcuffed to my past.

2. I forgive, and I will choose to remember no more.

3. I give up my right to avenge myself.

4. I forgive my ex-husband, I release him.

5. I must, and I will protect my mindset.

6. My forgiveness does not mean they were right.

7. I forgive because I was forgiven.

CHAPTER 7: **STARTING <u>YOU</u> ALL OVER AGAIN**

F ord Motor Company is an American icon. In the devastating financial crash of 2008, it was the one and only automobile manufacturer to bypass the government bailout. Instead of waiting out the crisis of 2008, they continued to move forward, stay innovative, invest, and rebuild Ford on an already firm and strategically designed foundation, principle set forth by Henry Ford. I would feel safe to say that Ford's CEO Alan Mulally's faith in recovery due to the preceding foundation prevailed in the end. CEO Mulally saw beyond the current dire circumstances (he had *vision*) and held the helm, knowing that the foundation that had been set was one of past, present, and future success. *(www.generalmotors.com)*

At one time, I was under the misconception that rebuilding my finances, emotions, and children's stability was not going to take a great effort. Growing up, I cannot recall being taught how to start over after a loss. I knew of financial issues in our business, but I did not know the details of how my parents rebuilt and ultimately rebounded from business setbacks. What I did know for sure is that they did not throw in the towel and quit—they came up with a new game plan to succeed, built on a firm foundation, and the business was sustained until the death of my stepfather nineteen years later.

Foundation

Foundation: A basis (as a tenet, principle, or axiom) upon which something stands or is supported, an underlying base or support. (Merriam-Webster Dictionary)

1 Kings 5:17 describes the building of a temple by King Solomon. *"And the king commanded, and they brought great stones, costly stones, and hewed stones, to lay the foundation of the house."*

A good architect must be chosen; one who visualizes and creates plans that can be built. This person will plan, design structures, and oversee the full construction process. The plans must have strategic measurements necessary to allow the vision to come to pass. It is the architect's job to find out what is required and develop a concept and a foolproof plan that can be built on a solid foundation, one that is built to last. Once the architect finishes his plans, the plans are then sent to the builder. The builder examines the plans and chooses the appropriate foundation. The builder would never use the foundation for a 2000 square-foot, contemporary style home as the foundation for a twenty-five-story skyscraper. The appropriate—and lifelong—foundation must be chosen and laid before the building process begins.

In 1906, most buildings and homes were built on landfills consisting of rocks, mud, and garbage. Sea-level areas were once a part of the Bay waters. What was not known at that time was that the land would inevitably lose its strength and stability through a liquefaction process. Garbage rots liquefies and softens over time. Landfills shake violently in earthquakes. It is not solid and cannot withstand any ground disturbance, so whatever is built on top of it moves without restraint. Disaster is unavoidable. Great destruction and fire were the residual effects of a poor foundation in the earthquake of 1906.

There are also homes and buildings in San Francisco that were built on bedrock, a unyielding and solid rock. These homes have withstood many earthquakes and to this day still, stand undamaged. In the 1989 Bay Area Loma Pieta earthquake, I was in an area of San Francisco built on bedrock, and I did not feel the earthquake because of the foundation the area rested on. A well-built building secured with the right plans may sway but will not break when the wind blows. When a more violent attack is imminent, and there is an underlying in-depth rumble, the structure may lose a few minor cosmetic details, but it will not crumble. It will still stand firm on its foundation.

Lives fall apart when the foundation upon which they were built needs to be re-laid.
~Iyanla Vanzant

Who Built the Foundation?

You must accept the fact that God knows your destiny. He knows what foundation is needed for your purpose in Him.

God will allow circumstances and situations to arise. These trials and tribulations are necessary to produce the real you. The fiery trials and the refiner's fire are there to remove the filth, dross, and stain of the world from His children. It's necessary to produce a substance used to lay a firm foundation for our purpose. God knows that once a thing is shed—a character flaw, a habit, an unhealthy desire—what lies behind it will come forth and bloom. It will be good and full of purpose. The purpose in our life is imminent. Living on purpose is a whole lot easier with the right foundation.

I had to stop fighting the process. The process has steps, and each step takes you closer to God by purification. I fought the process in ignorance. I didn't understand how these things could produce a new me when they had only angered and depressed me.

The foundation that I had begun to build my life upon was not firm—it was landfill material. My adult life and marriage had been built on damaged goods. It was packed dirt, garbage, and rocks and would not give strength to anything built upon it. My mind was cluttered, so in the process of trying to take control of my life, I had unknowingly and unintentionally created a new foundation which mirrored that of my past.

Ground Failure

Infidelity will shake you, the covenant now has ground failure, and what once stood tall and strong is now crumbled, a useless pile of debris. When the Bible discusses the building of a thing, it talks specifically about the foundation. It identifies what was being built and the specific materials it was laid with. It was always built with the best quality materials as the success of anything important starts with the right foundation.

The tearing down of a structure can be a lengthy, dirty, and tedious process. It can cause fatalities and is often not a pretty sight. Picture in your mind a building. The outside is freshly painted, bright and colorful, but it has been eaten from the inside out by termites. Now, the building is scheduled for destruction. A crane with a wrecking ball strikes it. It's shaken, and a large hole is left where the ball hit. The materials from that spot come crumbling down. But the rest of the building is still standing. If the building had a nervous system as we all do, it would be in great pain, still living and breathing. It is similar to us when the Lord has to tear us down and rebuild us. We may cry out, "What are you doing, Lord?"

"What sorrow awaits those who argue with their Creator? Does a clay pot argue with its maker? Does the clay dispute with the one who shapes it, saying, stop, you're doing it wrong" (Isaiah 45:9 NLT).

When He, the architect, and the builder see the work He once created has been marred, He must either redo it or destroy it all together. A few things could happen in the building process. The visionary shared his data/plan with the architect. Then he relayed the plans to the builder, but the manager of the project being built was not cooperative, and delayed the process, and demanded that things be done another way. Unfortunately, the manager's desires and direction are outside of the visionary's instructions. However, the foundation was laid correctly, so there would not be a reason to tear it apart, but the structure is weak and needs to be torn down and rebuilt to its original specifications. Spiritually, I had to allow God to tear down this structure and destroy the foundation, too, because my former foundation was built on pain and abuse. Now God can create an everlasting foundation to withstand and not break, even though it may sway. God created me to stand firm, not to crumble, but to endure (2 Timothy 2:3).

In times past, I have recorded quite a few interesting dreams. But this particular one seems to surface more often than others. In 1999, I had a dream of a level four tornado that was headed towards my home, a Victorian-style home similar to the ones with etched hillsides on the renowned Fell Street in the Fillmore district of San Francisco. My home was high up on a piece of land that sat above the other houses on the block. I could see over the rooftops of the houses facing my house and saw the storm coming afar off, raging, loud, and violent. It was destroying everything in its path. I gathered my children and my mother, ran out of the home, got into my car, and drove north to the top of a huge hill and looked down on the town as the tornado destroyed it. I saw that it was turning west and passing on by, but it never took its eyes off of me, as if its goal was to come my way. I got in my car and returned to my home, still at peace and still standing unmoved and in perfect condition. But everything around me was in shreds, totally destroyed. The next night, I dreamed it again. This time, I looked out of my big, beautiful window and saw the storm headed my way again. I gathered my children and mother, ran down the stairs and got into my car. I attempted to start the car, but it wouldn't start. I looked at the gas gauge and saw I was out of gas. We all looked up as the tornado moved closer in our direction. I could see it gnashing its teeth, eyes red and forehead furrowed. I continued to stare intensely, not in fear but solemnly. As it approached, I didn't hear any whistling or clashing, nor did I feel any rumbling or thunderous sounds. I didn't hear or feel anything. The car didn't sway, rock, or move at all. The tornado passed right in front of me and went north this time, straight up to the hill where I had run in the previous dream. It destroyed everything in its path, even the ground, and continued, watching me the entire time. I got out of my car, went back in the house, and closed the door slowly.

I had no idea back in 1999 that this dream would soon become a reality. However, as in the dream, no matter the intensity of the rage or violence launched against me, I remained standing unaffected. The path I had taken to escape was destroyed, and I no longer could run. I remained unscarred. I won.

I began to embrace the fact that this rebuilding was a prime opportunity for God's greatness in me to be revealed. No more rolling and wallowing on the floor when a problem arose. I allowed hard trials, tests, and mistakes to build my strength, character, and my faith in God. I began to rest in God. I had to tell myself daily that no one could defeat me but me. Defeat in Jesus was impossible.

I began to take on His Scriptures. I was determined to see me smiling back at me when I opened my Bible. Despite naysayers and the rejection of my family and friends, I became obedient and relentless in obtaining the life the Lord had purposed for me. I had to examine myself and allow the Lord to check my thoughts, motives, and intent. I endured my errors and shortcomings. Did I do everything right? Absolutely not. I made bad decisions, wrong moves, and bad choices. *But His grace was sufficient, and my weakness was made strong in Him.* I had to hear God, listen to His instructions, and put the instructions into action. There were times when God would give me a song, and it would continue to play in my mind. I recognized that it was God speaking to me, and I began to think of the lyrics to the song. Rebuilding is also a new way of thinking. You must change the way you think to be successful. You must play the hand you have been dealt. Don't give up—play to win. If your card is divorce, play it. See it as a fresh start and a new beginning. If it's bankruptcy, it's a new start and an opportunity to raise your credit score to its highest. If it's abuse, think about how you can speak out so that others will speak up. If you lost a loved one, start a foundation in their name. Do good so that others can be blessed. If it's financial hardship, find God's promise for your situation. Pray and believe in that promise. Act upon it. Take whatever your situation is and hit it head-on. Pull the good out of it, and accept the change as an opportunity for greatness.

Courage to Keep Going

I struggled, failed, and started again. Did I fall apart? Yes. Shrink back in fear? Yes. But my children's sanity depended on me. I had to look at the situations and realize they were going to make me stronger. I sought God, and I dealt with my fear of raising children as a single parent, and being "ALONE". Was every day a good day? Not by a Texas long shot. (if one exists) Most days were tough, but my determination was relentless. I was feeling strength I had never known. I became focused on the intent of glorifying God in every area of my life. I had much to gain by doing so. I had to accept my calling and embrace the woman God was making. I fought my way through insecurity, fear, and timidity to become the woman I am today. It was more than worth the fight to live in the precious victory that God had intended for my life all along.

Are you asking where can I begin? Right here, and right now. As you take a deep breath, here is some food for thought:

- Admit quickly. Often, we don't acknowledge that we are marred. Admittance is the first sign of strength, and yes, you are strong. Change is hard, but you must look beyond self-pity and low self-esteem to find the vision of what you will become. Don't ignore your crumbled, out-of-control emotions. They need to be restored and built upon a firm foundation.

- Ask yourself what you're afraid of losing. Honesty is key here. Usually, it's the loss we fear the most. Loss of identity, or control. Deal with strategy, seek solutions, and ask for help! Don't let pride or fear of "no" rob you of your impending success. Write, write, and did I say *write?* Write down your fears, face them, hate them, and destroy them. Don't ignore the sleepless nights, the lack of appetite, and the poor money management.

- Ask yourself, "How did I get here? And if I stay in this state, what is it costing me, where will I land in life?" What negative words and past experiences built your foundation?

- The truth is you were made by God. Self-destroying words like *I can't, I'm not worthy, I don't deserve, I can't accept, I don't fit* are just lies the enemy has planted in your ear. You hear them and subconsciously repeat them, owning the lie. The truth is just the opposite. What if you believed that you are worthy because God says that you are. What if you just took Him at His word? How would your life be? What do you see?

Truths:

1) A foundation can also be a principle upheld by your family. Hold tight. Buckle up.

2) The plans must have strategic measurements necessary to make the vision come to pass.

3) The builder takes the plans, examines them, and chooses the appropriate foundation.

4) Fighting the process will only delay your destiny.

CHAPTER 8: **GET A BIG VISION**

"Where there is no vision, the people perish: but he
that keepeth the law happy is he."
(Proverbs 29:18)

Vision is a beacon, a lighthouse beam that guides you
into purpose. ~Angela D. **Holmes**

D on't be moved at all by what you see—be moved only by what you believe. So, get a vision... Sit, think, and create a new you. Obey the purpose the Lord has called you to. Be deliberate and be intentional. Vision brings drive and determination. Look at the *POWER* of vision. Your thoughts of success have to be as close as your skin is to your body—inseparable. It can't be a far-fetched goal or indescribable idea. You have to taste it and make it tangible in your spirit; visualizing and speaking are powerful. A great life and future begin with a vision.

"And they said, Go to, let us build us a city, with a
tower whose top may reach unto heaven; and let us make
us a name lest we be scattered abroad upon the

face of the whole earth, And the Lord said, behold the people is one and they have all one language; and this they begin to do, and now nothing will be restrained from them which they have IMAGINED to do" (Genesis 11:4).

They said it and thought it. Visualized it and acted upon it. It was pure power that brought the vision to pass. The Lord created and ordained the power in our tongues and our minds. The Lord used vision and agreement as the covenant with Abram.

"And he brought him forth abroad and said Look now toward heaven and tell the stars if thou be able to number them sand he said unto him, so shall thy seed be, and he believed in the Lord, and he counted it to him for righteousness" (Genesis 15:5-5.)

Can you visualize Abram looking up at a still, black night, and a massive number of stars to behold? I've always visualized Abram smiling and gazing in awe and wonder. Your vision and your perspective on any given situation are really the core of who you are. Vision was the part of my healing process that brought relief and a sense of purpose in my life. There were days of depression and sulking, and days when I blamed everyone, I knew for my feelings of abandonment and loneliness. My mind was in a state of depression. I could not see the good in my life. I had no vision and could not see my future. I made mistakes—major ones—and made bad money choices (e.g. emotional spending and prideful spending). But eventually, I allowed God to correct me.

"Apply thine heart unto instruction, and thine ears to the words of knowledge" (Proverbs 23:12).

In doing this, you will begin to see what God sees in you. Can you envision your life healed? Can you see what you are missing by staying in misery. You have the power to choose! I discovered that what we think can heal us—or kill us. One day, I realized that four years had gone by, and I couldn't account for those years. It was a complete blur. It was as if I was in a paddle boat with one oar, continually swirling in a circle. Without vision, life stands still; it doesn't move. I began to think about being and becoming more than I ever had been in my life. I painted a picture in my mind and visualized being healed, set free, and being successful. I wanted everything that God promised in my life.

"For I know the thoughts that I think toward you, saith the LORD, thoughts of peace, and not of evil, to give you an expected end" (Jeremiah 29:11).

I chose to find me. I wanted to believe what I could not see, let alone do for myself. I had to realize God was not angry with me, He does not hate me because I am divorced. I don't have to weak sackcloth and ashes for the rest of my life. But that I have a great and awesome future planned for me. I had to understand that things don't just happen, they are intentional and purposeful. I began to see a glimpse of a future that I had never seen. I saw a person in myself that I didn't know—she was whole, peaceful and complete and she lacked nothing. She was full of integrity, she was creative, she was beautiful inside, and she was fruitful and washed clean of her past. She was a vessel that the Master had chosen as His own. She was not chosen by the world but loved and chosen by God. God began to open my eyes. What had been clouded before was now clear. The woman I saw had a purpose. She had been called by God to do great work in His kingdom. She looked at me and smiled, and I looked at her and rejoiced. I said to myself, *"I will not stop. I am going to fight."*

Success is due to our stretching to the challenges of life.
Failure comes when we shrink from them.
~John Maxwell

Now I was grabbing hold of vision, and it caused my blood to run warm again and my body to heal. There is an enormous amount of documented and successful vision-driven Scriptures in the Bible, which make it evident that the Lord knows to obtain a substantial, lasting change of mind. It all starts with a vision. This change of mind alters our destiny and shakes us right back onto our intended path. We were created to visualize, write, obtain, and subdue. God is moved by faith and faith only.

Take Courage

God speaks to us through visions. Take a moment while awake to meditate and visualize your future. You must see yourself outside of the label and stigma of divorcee. I am sick of condemning categories wrongfully used by society. Be honest with God. Take your heart and place it in His hands. He already knows everything you're feeling, and He's waiting for you with open arms.

Visualization and affirmations begin and end in your mind. It is not the end until you are mentally victorious over the situation. An affirmation is personal, and it's positive. It's now, and it's at the moment, and you must visualize it and see it. You agree with the Word of God concerning your life. You should be able to touch it and describe it with passion in vivid detail.

Now, it's time to write. Writing your vision changes everything. It becomes alive, and you will find yourself transforming your very life to obtain it. Set goals with actual dates. The Bible tells us in Ephesians 5:16 *"to make the best of every day, using each day to its full purpose".*

The empires of the future are the empires of the mind.
~Winston Churchill

Think about this…I heard about a man who went to deliver a package to a tattoo parlor, and as he stood and looked through the tattoos of past customers, he came across one that said, "Born to lose." The delivery guy asked the tattoo technician, "Did someone really get this tattooed on their body?" The technician said, "Yes, tattooed on his mind first, then tattooed on his body." Wow!

Vision is critical and powerful. Our history has shaped our mindset. An unhealthy mindset is what I had to break. I had to fight weakness, failure, family dysfunction, abuse, and destructive ways—all of which kept me from dreaming, hoping, and visualizing. It kept me from *becoming*.

Go Forward

When the children of Israel made an exodus from Egypt (Exodus 13), they spoiled the Egyptians and left with more than they had. Well, that victory brought a little situation called the Red Sea. When they saw the sea, they angrily came against Moses, and he tried to still the people by assuring them that God would fight for them. "Fear not!" He said.

"The Lord said to Moses why do you cry to me? Tell the people of Israel to go forward"
(Exodus 14:15, ESV).

Regardless of what I was faced with, I had to keep my vision before me. You must have a vision of the future, not your past. The past for the Israelites was slavery and pain. Stay out of pain's corridor, use what you have in your hand. It works. Go forward in life. Don't lie down and allow the devil to trample you. I had to admit that my life's baggage was trash, and it only allowed me to be trampled on.

I had to leave it behind and visualize the newness of life as I was starting over. You must press to make life what you want it to be. If you don't have an idea as to what you want to do, pray for purpose until it is revealed. Research your passions and spend time finding out who you are. God has a purpose for you. Keep moving and do something. Write, write, and write. Write the things that represent the pain or challenge in your life on the left side of a piece of paper. Draw a line down the center of the paper, and on the right-hand side, write the good that you can pull out of it. It is good in every situation we face.

"We are assured and know that (God being a partner in their labor) all things work together and are (fitting into a plan) for good to and for those who love God and are called according to (His) design and purpose"
(Romans 8:28, AMP).

That means you! Reach out for help. Don't let pride keep you hungry, broke, and lonely. Don't be idle. Depression can and will set in. Days and years will pass, and all the purpose, gifts, passions, and desires that the Lord put in you to enjoy will waste away, and that is NOT His intent for your life. John 10:10 clearly describes the destruction the devil will wreak on a wasted nonproductive life. It says he comes to do three major things—kill, steal, and destroy.

"The thief's purpose is to steal and kill and destroy. My purpose is to give them a rich and satisfying life" (John 10:10, NLT). This Scripture gives the emphasis of MORE. It describes God's desire for the abundance He wants to give us. Your outlook and your perspective are what makes the difference. When I saw only shame, pain and divorce, I did not see a future. My thoughts were bleak, and my eyes were dim. I was so blinded by shame that I did not have the desire to dream, to think ahead, to plan, or to set a goal.

God never gives us instructions without telling us how to do it and how He is going to bless us for our obedience to the Scriptures. He provides us with the Kingdom's keys to success. I was painfully full of pride. I had never had to struggle financially. I had what I needed and wanted, and if I didn't, I knew how to get it. I wasn't living by faith but by *"tip-toe faith"* as Bishop I.V. Hilliard says. This was how the Lord began to change my perspective, my outlook on my life, and what I thought about divorce. My visualizations and daily affirmations began with the end of the matter in mind, my expected end.

"Better is the end of a thing than the beginning thereof;
and the patient in spirit is better than the proud in spirit"
(Ecclesiastes 7:8).

I wondered why this was taking so long. I had lots of questions, and I was sick of being sick and tired. But the Lord continued to rebuild me. I would often hear a Scripture and conceive what He was saying to me. I had to realize that the Lord had already established my success in the beginning, and I had to get through the process. Remember this is not a surprise to God.

"Declaring the end and the result from the beginning,
and from ancient times the things that are not yet done,
saying, My counsel shall stand, and I will do all My
pleasure and purpose" (Isaiah 46:10, AMP).

Jeremiah 29:11 says, *"For I know the thoughts that I think toward you, saith the LORD, thoughts of peace, and not of evil, to give you an expected end."* What was my expected end? I realized that I was just floating through time, inhaling and exhaling on a daily basis. I didn't exist, I was numb, and life was bleak. I listened to the devil's lies that my life did not matter, that the end was destruction. Poverty was trying to take over in my spirit and my natural life. This was becoming a reality because I did not have a vision. I had to take back my mind. I became determined not to waste this good life that the Lord so graciously blessed me with. Why would I lay down and die when I could LIVE, be whole, and prosper in Christ Jesus? Provision was already made for me on the cross when Jesus shed His precious blood. I had, to begin with the end in mind. Angela, your end is not the end until you are mentally victorious over the situation. When you change that, girlfriend, you have WON! Things may not yet have changed, but my outlook, my VISION, and joy for the promise are what *lifted* me out of the mud. I had to stop making life hard for myself. Jesus' grace was my rest and resolve. He chose me and was responsible for my end. He determined my ending in the beginning.

This is so important—we must know and understand that this life and its situations have already been handled, and the victory in every situation is already won. Even when I did not see an immediate move of God in my situation and did not know when the end would come, through tears and talking to myself, I pressed on through every day. I printed pictures, wrote sticky notes, posted and pasted whatever it took for me to visualize my future through God's Word. I often said, "This can't be it—this is not God's destiny for me. I refuse to believe it." I started to visualize all that I could do and be. Visualize what you speak, and you must say something—you may not trust or have faith in yourself, but trust and speak God's Word.

What Are You Affirming Daily?

What are you speaking, and what do you see with your heart? Speak God's Word and agree with it. I had to picture myself happy, joyful, at peace, lacking nothing. I described in detail what I desired and what I believed according to God's Word concerning my children's lives and my own. Your vision has to be mentally tangible. Touch it with your mind and describe it intensely and with passion. Make provisions to make room for it. You have to think about whatever it is that brings anxiety and doubt in your mind. Yes, you must think about it to master it. See the situation, the feeling, or the circumstance, and remember how you are handling it and how it is making you feel right now. Then take the Word of God and handle it. Play it out as a script in your mind—see yourself overachieving, overpowering, and mastering your emotions and the situation until you have a heartfelt and visual victory. Do it until your behavior changes. Don't give up! Pray until there is change. I said to myself, *"Angela if you do nothing, you will be nothing. If you don't ever try, you will never succeed".*

The success, which is the testimony, does not stop. It's not, "Hey, I beat depression, and now it's over." No, your drive to fight your way out of depression has to govern *all* areas of your life. You have to improve *you* to stay out of depression. The strength that God gives to us to overcome something is not just for that situation—but it is, in fact, a tool to fight the enemy for the rest of our lives. Fighting the residuals of divorce is not pretty. Once you overcome and conquer ground, it's yours. As my beloved Pastor, Tamara Bennett said, *"Saints should be on the offense, not the defense running from Satan."* In essence, we should control the court. When that enemy invades our territory, we are to drive the devil out by force, annihilate him, and utterly destroy him by being vision-driven.

Again, Proverbs 23:7 says, *"For as he thinketh in his heart, so is he."* What do you think about you? What do you think drives your character, your ways, and your actions? Is what is in your heart evil or good? Or are you thinking you are not loveable, ugly, unfit, rejected and a cast away? This is no time for a pity party—be strong. What have you made preparations for? Are you prepared to succeed? Do you expect God's best in spite of your past or current situation? Don't let life's events dictate your future.

I had to see and feel my happiness and joy. I internalized the vision so much that just thinking about it made me giddy. I felt the love I had always desired. I visualized it until it was real, and the loneliness departed. Your life will not change until you get a true vision, and get a big one. See big—look through God's eyes. Even in our mistakes, we need to see the forgiveness and correction of our Father and see His blessing in it. Don't limit yourself to your present situation, feeling, or state of mind. Darkness dulls your understanding, and if you cannot see a greater you, you will not press beyond your obstacles.

Ask yourself the following questions:

- Who do you see, and whom do you want others to see?
- How do you carry yourself?
- How do you feel about yourself?
- What image are you portraying?
- Do you look and feel as if life has run you over full speed? When people see you, do they see a sad, broken, and hurt person or a confident and motivated individual who loves life?

- Are your actions healthy, full of integrity, and character?

- Do you respect yourself?

- What vision do you have for yourself?

- Are you valuable or a liability?

Your image speaks volumes about you! Vision will cause you to be strengthened, hold your head up, square your shoulders, and fight the good fight of faith. How do you want to be seen or approached? Realize and affirm that you are a winner, and failure is not a part of your DNA. My vision became bigger than what was around me and bigger than who was around me. My vision was even greater than my past. In the past, it was so hard to think and dream magnificent things. It was my way of thinking—as a child, I did not dream big and reach for the sky, so it was hard for me to see beyond my situations and circumstances. Many days I felt as if I would never start over, but those were the days when I took a long, hard look in the mirror and aggressively worked to change what and who I saw. I had to renew me, renew my image of myself. I did not want to look like "her" (the old me), walk like her, or even dress like her. I had to allow God to renew my image, by renewing my mind with new vision.

"And be constantly renewed in the spirit of your mind [having a
fresh mental and spiritual attitude]"
(Ephesians 4:23, AMP).

Get a vision, dream it, pursue it, and subdue, and grab hold of it with your whole heart. Relying on your past or even present state will not allow you to move forward. So, let go of the past! Success happens if you live in it. Get a vision, and get your life back!

Like a storm victim clinging to a tree in the middle of
hurricane-force winds; cling to the hope that your vision
will become reality. Never let go!
~Dr. Teresa Hairston

Truths:
1) Vision takes courage. You got this.
2) Vision gives a hope of a better tomorrow. You deserve it.
3) Writing your vision brings it to life.
4) Look at it, read, and touch your vision daily. This will produce maximum results.
5) God is behind your vision—He gave it to you!

Start Now!

Get a vision board and dream, research, print, and paste. Date your desired goals and get excited about the new life you are forming right before your eyes. You can use the space below to map out some ideas.

NOTES: Write down what you are determined to change in your life, based on these truths.

_____

_____

_____

_____

_____

_____

_____

_____

_____

_____

_____

_____

_____

_____

_____

_____

_____

_____

_____

_____

_____

_____

_____

CHAPTER 9: **LEARNING TO TRUST AGAIN**

The moment there is suspicion about a person's motives,
everything he does becomes tainted.
~Mahatma Gandhi

One thing which, if removed, will destroy the most
powerful government, business, economy, leadership, the
greatest friendship, character, the deepest love; That one
thing is trust. ~Stephen M. R. Covey

Forgiveness is a gift, but trust is earned.
~Angela D. Holmes

Strength – Seeing and accepting the big picture, admittance and a mindset for change

Obstacle – Isolation, fear of failure, low self-esteem, suspicion

Overcoming – Prayer, praise, purpose, vision

Trust – Assured reliance on the character, ability, strength, or truth of someone or something, dependence on one in whom confidence is placed. Trust is a process that allows you to rest your emotional judgment toward that person, group, or idea.

My life was so hectic with emotional attacks that I began to lose trust in humanity. I thought everyone was out to misuse and mistreat me and that there was no one to trust. I believed if I was out buying tires, the merchants were crooks. In the grocery store, they were crooks, too. I didn't trust my coworkers, people I associated with, and most definitely my immediate family. I had so many secrets and pains that had been undealt with, that when I did reach out, I expected that rejection and betrayal would soon follow. My mind continually revisited the rejection of my family, the betrayal of my ex-husband, and the wrongs that were never made right. My belief that loyalty and sincerity still existed was nonexistent. Trust? No way, not here. Truthfully, trust is difficult and time-consuming to build up but can be easily destroyed quickly.

I didn't allow anyone to get too close to me, and I removed myself at the slightest sign of betrayal or vacillation in conduct or personality. I thought I was better off alone because I didn't know who to trust, and based on my past experiences, having the ability to trust in the future was not promising.

I had trusted my stepfather, and my ex-husband with my heart and these important people in my life destroyed a very vulnerable mind and had severely and negatively impacted my ability to reason. I thought that if *they* could hurt me, then who could I trust? I had given my heart to my ex-husband, and he had broken my trust. I had stood by my mother's side, and when she pushed me away, I was crushed and confused. I had trusted the words of my stepfather, but he was manipulating, mind controlling, and seducing.

I was so lost and sought solitude, building a greater wall around me to keep people out. I was genuinely confused and bewildered. I sat on my wall, ready to protect me, ready for war. Men became the enemy. Every look and every stare were torn apart with my bitter, resentful eye, purposely intended to make them look the other way. When I looked at men, I saw only adulterers and fools, cheaters, cowards who lacked integrity and were only out to harm. I had resolved in my mind that men were weak, and women were catty, manipulative and not worthy of trust. My thoughts of remarrying were always cut short because I could not find a place in my mind where I believed that someone could be faithful to me. My trust was shattered. I remained convinced

I could never trust again. I became angry with *me*—I had allowed myself to be tricked and had allowed a man to rip my emotions to pieces. I gave up ground that I never should have and let someone hold my emotions at bay.

How could I ever trust again?

The fear of reliving the past pain in my life caused me a great deal of distress. I had to make a choice and come to the conclusion that this distrustful spirit was controlling me. I was going to allow God to take complete control, or I was going to remain in a dismal state of distrust. I was afraid of life and afraid to be hurt again, spooked and full of fear, thinking the world was against me, but it was time to stop hiding and fight. The Lord often pulled me into prayer, and I would hear the words, "Trust me, you will never see this trial again." I would scream with desperation at the top of my lungs like a newborn baby, "I trust you; Lord, help me!"

Trust is the one thing that changes everything.
~Stephen M. R. Covey

Take A Look at Yourself

This truth was very crucial for me to understand. Learning to trust again after infidelity and betrayal is difficult but not impossible. Learning to trust God and trust yourself will kick-start your personal growth and development. Your trust will be rebuilt, but the extent will depend on the sensitivity of the betrayal. You will have a hesitancy to believe people without proof of their character. Trust can often be repaired through sincere, verbal admittance to breaking trust, by honesty and a change of behavior. My grandmother would always say you could trust a thief, but not a liar. Why? Because you already know what the thief is going to do if you allow him or her to do it. But a liar is deceitful and tricky.

In a traumatic situation that has caused loss of trust, we often seek an explanation and details from the dishonest party. For some reason, we think that their account will be truthful. Once we realize that their answers to our questions were also lies, we turn into detectives, searching for a truth that we really don't want. This makes the road to healing convoluted. After all, is said and done, our real issue is, can we trust our judgment of character, and can we make wise decisions in the future?

I read an article that described various steps in rebuilding trust after an affair has ended. In my situation, my ex-husband's affair never ended, but trust after infidelity *can* be rebuilt, and you can go on to have a healthy, thriving, more vibrant marriage. But *both* parties have to agree to these terms. Trusting should always be done with realistic expectations, and knowing a person's past and present characteristics will aid in trusting. Don't be afraid.

Trusting God with my relationships was the first step. Trusting that I could be a good judge of character and rest in my decisions is growth. God showed me that, through circumstances and situations, my trust in Him would be built—not by my words only, but also by my actions. Was it easy? No, not by a long shot.

"What time I am afraid, I will have confidence in and put my trust and reliance in you"
(Psalm 56:3, AMP).

As the Lord began to reveal the plethora of areas in which I needed healing, trust stood out as a major one. Faith is the crowning glory of our walk with Christ. I had to have faith, to trust and believe that my heart was in the Master's hands. As I gave my heart to God and allowed God to build a firm foundation, I had to trust God in everything, even when following His plan didn't make sense. God will never leave us or forsake us. He knows the who, what, where, and why of all situations. He knows why we should establish relationships or detach from them. He will warn us. That inner voice and your instinct is God's guidance. Trusting God with your relationships is foolproof.

> *Fears are nothing more than a state of mind.*
> *~Napoleon Hill*

God gives us practical daily instructions and principles that He knows are foolproof; however, we overlook and disobey. We think it's too easy; that it has to be something huge and hard.

Let me interject: When God says to put our trust and reliance in Him and not on man, are we really doing that? Unbelief is a lack of trust. When you read or hear God's Word, what are your actions demonstrating to God; trust or distrust? When we are in the middle of a great emotional battle, we begin to think that our freedom from this issue is far-fetched and unattainable. How wrong we are.

"But I trust in thee, O Lord; I said, thou art my God. My times are in thy hand"
(Psalm 31:14-15, KJV).

Our deliverance has perfect timing—God is never late, slow, or forgetful. I had to learn to rely on God totally, and this began to build my trust in Him first. I could not allow pain to disconnect me from the Lord, the one who held my success and the one who loved and truly cared for me. Unfortunate situations were by no means surprises or "oops" moments to God—I had to love, envision, and embrace the fact that it was ultimately all for my good.

It pays to trust God with all and to make no reservations.
~Smith Wigglesworth

Are You Trustworthy?

No matter what the cause of distrust in your life, you must learn to trust God and live an abundant life. Throughout the Word of God, we find many Scriptures on trusting God—*not man*—with our cares, needs, and desires. Becoming distant and secluding yourself is not the answer to your lack of trust. The answer is in the Lord. Be honest with yourself, especially if *you* have not been a very trustworthy person.

Never enter any deals, partnerships, or friendships without first seeking God. People you encounter at this point in your life have a purpose in your life, be it for good or for evil.

Prayer: *Lord I trust you with all my relationships, move those that mean harm and pull close those who are sent by you.*

You are in control of what you think and how you behave. You are responsible for your actions. Your behavior speaks volumes. How and whom you trust will depend on your perspective and your outlook on life.

You see, we must trust that God will lead and guide us in all things. The choices to place trust where we were not supposed to and to the degree that was never intended were things that *we* chose to do, not God. The Lord puts people in our lives to assist us in many facets of our lives, mainly to fulfill the purpose God intends for your life. He also puts you in the path of those that you are supposed to help. What if those people come into your life, but because you are full of distrust, you ignore them and push them away? The spouse you seek must be ordained and purposed by God you are to enhance each other and assist with purpose. You have a right to peace and happiness, so take it; it's yours! Just as I did, we often seek God for help in a matter, and God answers us, but because our idea of help isn't the same as His idea, we don't like what is in front of us, and blame God. This lack of trust stems from a lack of faith. Don't let your past offenses continue to control you. Realize that God does not do anything in a disorderly fashion. He is systematic, precise, and accurate—and His timing is perfect.

When He releases His blessing and intent for our lives, it goes to work immediately. His word directs our steps and keeps us on a track we may not even know we're on. Whatever the situation, your life is calculated to bring an "expected end." The pain, betrayal, healing, and blessing are all timely. It's all part of the plan, a part of the process. Healing brings trust, and this trust is the path to our blessing. Learning to trust again will mature us and allow us to not hold unreal expectations of people.

In any relationship, we must find the ability and the integrity to make things right. We must right our wrongs. When we have been hurt, and there was no closure to the offense, we can quickly become bitter and fearful of our future and relationships. If you take the Word of God and apply it to a situation when you are feeling this way, you will be able to live a healthy, trusting, and happy life. The answer is in God's word. It will tell you how and where to place your trust. It will let you know the areas of your life you need to change to become someone trustworthy and dependable with good morals and high integrity.

We must learn how to have healthy relationships. Don't stop your life based on past experiences with damaged relationships! Take those experiences and learn from them. Trust stems from our personal history in dealing with people and is influenced by the people around us, by media, by other cultures, and by society. There are clear, undeniable areas of trust that you must have to have healthy relationships. Every day we create and invent new things or ideas. At the end of each day, we are responsible for how we utilized that day for the worth it had (Ephesians 5:15-17, AMP).

Harboring a lack of trust depletes energy, personal drive, and a willingness to forgive, and it fosters a dark atmosphere of heightened suspicion. Won't you allow God to take your worst situation and make it beautiful? He has a purpose for your life, and He can bring forth beauty from the pain. You will heal unscarred.

CHAPTER 10:

PRAYER STRATEGY TO WIN

Prayer—Our intimate way of communication with God. He longs for our prayers.

"Now Jesus was telling the disciples a parable to make the point that at all times they ought to pray and not give up and lose heart," (Luke 18:1, AMP).

Don't bother to give God instructions; just report for duty~ Corrie ten Boom

Matthew 21:22 states, "And all things, whatsoever ye shall ask in prayer, believing, ye shall receive." Pray with confidence, pray God's Word, confess it, and proclaim it. Decree His Word and speak faith only. Proverbs 18:21 tells us that "life and death are in the power of the tongue." Don't you know that faith is released through our words? When we speak God's words, we are speaking His thoughts which are His will. Speaking and praying God's Word will manifest and yield powerful results. We can only pray effectively when we know the Word of God for any given situation. God's Word will annihilate strongholds, demolish and break to pieces the works of the enemy in our lives and others.

When I began to work for the Department of Veteran Affairs in 2006, I asked the Lord why. What is my purpose in this agency? What are you showing me? He began to give me analogies of missiles and bombs, of what they do and why. He showed me a guided missile and explained to me how it was calculated for a particular target. It would not hit anything but its intended target—it would not hit planes or bridges. The calculations for the missile were set, and it carried them out by any means necessary. He said that is how I want your prayers to be. I was clueless but said "Okay," and went on with life. This is how He wanted me to approach prayer. He wanted it to become my way of life, a part of my purpose. He began to show me various branches of the American military and what they do, who does what first and why. These represented the positioning of the saints of God who war in prayer. Prayer must be a *first* in your life, an essential component that starts takes you through and ends each day.

Special Forces

There is a time to be an ambassador and a time to be a soldier. You must gain the skill set to engage your enemy.

The Marines are a highly mobile attack force that can function either in water or on dry land. Their goal is to take the territory, and they are usually sent in first for a reason. They have been highly trained and have special techniques—they go in, take control of the situation, and paralyze the enemy. The Army then moves in to maintain control and possession of the area. There are special forces for special missions. And so it is with the saints of the High God. We must find out our positioning in warfare and prayer, accept it and perfect it.

"Wherefore the rather, brethren, give diligence to make your calling and election sure: for if ye do these things, ye shall never fall" (2 Peter 1:10).

Are you a member of the Special Forces who comes in strong against territories, regions, and areas? Are you a first responder, one who gets a call and immediately goes into prayer? Are you ground force, showing up on the scene and pleading the blood of Jesus in hospital rooms and other emergency situations? Do you have all-night binding prayers? We all have a place in prayer. Find yours, perfect it, and submit it to God. There is a real war in the spirit! Don't go missing in action—we need you. I had to free myself from captivity and get on the battlefield in prayer. Know your enemy's ways just as he knows yours! Hit the devil on every turn, calculate the force and weaponry needed for deliverance. Your prayer matters! Check out these powerful Scriptures:

"And when he had taken the book, the four beasts and four and twenty elders fell down before the Lamb, having every one of them harps, and golden vials full of odors, which are the prayers of saints" (Revelation 5:8).

"And another angel came and stood at the altar having a golden censer; and there was given unto him much incense, that he should offer it with the prayers of all saints upon the golden altar which was before the throne" (Revelation 8:3).

"And the smoke of the incense, which came with the prayers of the saints ascended up before God out of the angel's hand" (Revelation 8:4).

CHAPTER 11: **LIVE ON PURPOSE**

My pain has brought forth my purpose. Where there is pain, there is always purpose. There is something coming forth. Adversity makes us strong—it has certainly made me strong. My tribulations were not meant to destroy me, but to strengthen me. You could not have told me my life would take the path that it took, but the hardness, the storms, and the heaviness all revealed my purpose—to reach out to others with kingdom-building tools. I have learned not to place a question mark on trouble, and I have learned not to question when God has placed a period on a situation. God is merciful and loving and ready to forgive. Without pain, we would have no compassion for others' faults, mishaps, and failures. Everything that happens to us is a resource for our purpose. You have the tools, authority, and power to fulfill your purpose.

What is My Purpose?

"The heart of man plans his way, but the Lord establishes his step" (Proverbs 16:9).

That answer begins with God. You find yourself resting in God when you live on purpose. Life is easier when you are on course with God's plan for your life, and you will quickly find out it's the only way to live. When we try and search for this answer in ourselves or a ten-step program, we will fail. No one knows your purpose but God. If you ask anyone who is truly operating in their purpose, they will tell you that who they are and what they are doing now is far from what they thought they would be doing in their life. Your God-given purpose brings meaning to our life. You live to connect with God daily, and you thirst to affect the lives of others with your purpose. You were not meant to live a mundane and mediocre life. God did not put that in your purpose.

Purpose will make you:
1) A highly effective person—whatever you touch will prosper. God meant it to be that way.
2) Increase in your faith. You were created on purpose with an intended purpose.
3) Happier, livelier, and determined to please God.

So, live out your life with impact and purpose. Living beneath your purpose and worth is a self-inflicted wound. Don't fight the blows, the hurts, and the rough moments, instead find purpose in everything you do, even in your darkest moments.

What was so painful in your past, had so much purpose. You have an intentional destiny, so pick up the shattered pieces of your past, and take a good look at them. Allow God to show you your purpose through your brokenness. Then allow Him to heal you, unscarred.

I want to live on purpose to the degree that my **every** *waking moment stills the enemy.*
~Angela D. Holmes

Matthew 16:19 states, "And I will give unto thee the keys of the kingdom of Heaven." These keys (tools) are critical and will unlock the shackles of the devil's strongholds on God's people. My purpose is to build women from the ruins of pain and despair with the tools that the Lord has given me. I am called to warfare in prayer. I so did not know that this was the direction in which the Lord was taking my life.

"And thou, O tower of the flock, the strong hold of the daughter of Zion, unto thee shall it come, even the first

dominion; the kingdom shall come to the daughter of Jerusalem" (Micah 4:8).

In 2009, my journey began my purpose, but at the time, I did not know the extent of this transition. I had a dream; a very realistic, clear, and relatively simple, yet revealing dream. In the dream, my spirit was saying that I just wanted to just enjoy life by sitting, smiling, and giving good hugs and words of encouragement to people. I settled my spirit and rested, and I was content and happy. I was sitting on a very crisp and clean beach. The sand was a perfect shade of tan, and the sky was the prettiest blue that I had ever seen. The weather was perfect, and the water was a deep dark blue, clean and refreshing. As the water touched the shore, it made a quiet tinkling sound. There were no clouds in the sky, and the air was still. I sat on the shore in a long, white linen dress—it was very pretty and had a stock attached. I sat with my arms wrapped just below my kneecaps, my knees pulled to my chin. I laid my head on my knees and thought to myself; _This is so pretty, so peaceful. I'm so happy. I never want to leave this place._

I looked straight ahead and was a little disturbed to see fog hovering over a small section of the ocean, but I tried to ignore it. I saw six men standing in the water, and they kept staring at me blankly, emotionless. They would turn their heads to do something in the fog then look at me again. *Where did the fog come from? Why are those men in the fog, and why do they keep staring at me? I* said to myself. It didn't make sense. Then suddenly, one of the men appeared on the shore where I was. He was holding a very ugly and slimy fish, one of the most disgusting fish I have ever seen. Its teeth were pointed and sharp, and they were exposed because it had no lips. *Why is he holding that disgusting fish? What is he doing?* He was intruding on my happy, clean moment. Without taking his eyes off of me, he lifted the fish and cut its belly open. My face clinched in disbelief. When he cut the belly open, the most beautiful iridescent pearls came pouring out, flowing slow and thick like waves of heavy cream.

In awe, I jumped to my feet and ran over to the man and began to scoop up the pearls into my smock, trying not to leave any behind. I couldn't believe these beautiful pearls had come out of this ugly disgusting fish. I embraced the pearls, one arm swaddled beneath and the other wrapped around and gripping the top in a protective way as if I was holding a baby in a large pouch in front of me. I looked over my shoulders from side to side protecting what I had in my arms and then quickly left the beach. Everyone in the dream watched me as I left. I woke up and remembered the dream and immediately wrote it down. I began to ask God about it. What did it mean?

Well, the dream itself was so full of my life that God had to reveal it to me piece by piece. The major part of the dream was you! Yes, you! You are the pearls that I so preciously cared for, created by God. When I asked God specifically about the pearls, He said, "My people are the fish, and they can get very dirty—even filthy—but they are full of pearls. Angela, love my people; they are precious to me." It's undeniable that the Lord has given me a heart for His people and indignation for the evilness and theft of souls that the enemy had committed. My watchfulness and looking over my shoulder represented the intercession for the souls, the pearls. My pain and purpose are for your deliverance and healing. Be delivered, be healed, and be set free. Today, after it all I am unscarred. As Christ is, so am I.

Make your work to be in keeping with your purpose.
~Leonardo da Vinci

AFFIRMATIONS

To state positivity; to state emphatically; to make known formally, officially, or explicitly; to make evident (Put the devil on notice; check him!)

- I am a success; I will succeed at whatever I put my hands too; I will follow God's formula for success. (Psalm 1:3, 2 Chronicles 26:5)

- I will never give up; I will see the results of God's promises in my life. (Romans 12:11)

- I have overcoming faith to change my life for the better. (1 John 5:4)

- I matter, and I am loved. (John 15:9)

- The Lord will never allow me to go hungry; He has given me diligent hands. (Proverbs 10:3-4)

- I am forever prosperous, and I have no lack because I serve and obey the Lord. (Job 36:11, Psalm 34:9-10)

- The attitude of my mind dictates my conduct; therefore, I will think right. (Philippians 4:8-9)

- My emotions are healed; this process is sealing my victory. (Isaiah 53:5)

- I am no longer bound by my past. I am safe with God. (1 John 3:21, Romans 8:1, Proverbs 18:10)

- I am an overcomer. I will not let hurt, pain, divorce, physical or mental abuse, molestation, incest, and rejection overtake me, but I will bind the powers of darkness that will try to keep me emotionally tied. (Matthew 16:19, John 15:26, Isaiah 61:3, Luke 10:13)

- The devil does not have a joint tenancy in my soul. There is a sole proprietor and owner, and that is my Lord and Savior Jesus Christ. (Romans 8:9, 2 Corinthians 6:16, 1 John 4:13)

- There is no double jeopardy. Christ already paid the price for my sins; once and for all, I am forgiven. (1 Corinthians 6:20)

- God has given me power to conquer through the blood of Jesus the mental attacks of the enemy. (James 4:7, Luke 10:13)

- I have power and authority to cast the devil out of my children, husband, family, friends and every situation he creeps into. (Matthew 10:1)

- I am blessed and not cursed, healed and delivered from weakness and persecutions. (Matthew 5:1-12)

- Anxiety is defeated. (Philippians 4:6)

- I have the power to become all that the Lord has intended for me to be. (Philippians 1:6)

- I will not fear, I have a vibrant efficient and purposeful life. (Romans 8:15)

- I am a powerful, praying woman of God, a Daughter of Zion. (Micah 4:8)

- I will always pray, giving God thanks in all things. (1 Thessalonians 5:18)

- God always hears my prayers; I will confess God's truths. (John 11:41-42, John 16:13)

- My prayers are important to God. (Revelation 8:3)

- My mind is healthy and vibrant. (2 Timothy 1:7)

- I speak life and not death; I will love and not hate. (Proverbs 15:4, Proverbs 18:21, Ephesians 5:2)

- I will renew my mind daily. (Romans 12:2, Ephesians 4:23)

- I will forgive and forget; just as God blots out my sins, so will I blot out all offenses committed against me. (Psalm 51:1,9)

RESOURCES

PEACE and a SOUND MIND

- *John 14:27* "Peace I leave with you, my peace I give unto you not as the world giveth, give I unto you. Let not your heart be troubled, neither let it be afraid."
- *Isaiah 26:3"* Thou wilt keep him in perfect peace, who's mind is stayed on thee because he trusteth in thee."

I bind and cast out spirits of hatred, bitterness, resentment, violence, unforgiveness, anger, retaliation, paranoia, suspicion, distrust, confrontation, and fear in the name of Jesus.

I bind and cast out all spirits of guilt, low self-esteem, shame, condemnation, and poverty in the name of Jesus.

PRAYER

- *Luke 18:1* "And he spake a parable unto them to this end, that men ought always to pray, and not to faint."

- *Philippians 4:6* "Be careful for nothing; but in everything by prayer and supplication with thanksgiving let your requests be made known unto God."

- *John 11:41-42* "Father, I thank You that You have heard me; Yes, I know You always hear and listen to me."

FORGIVENESS

- *Matthew 6:14* "For if you forgive men their trespasses, your heavenly Father will also forgive you."

- *Mark 11:25 (AMP)* "And whenever you stand praying, if you have anything against anyone, forgive him and let it drop (leave it, let it go), in order that your Father who is in heaven may also forgive you your[own] failings and shortcomings and let them drop."

- *Romans 3:23* "For all have sinned and come short of the glory of God."

HEALING and DELIVERANCE

- *Psalm 107:6* "Lord deliver me out of all my distresses"

- *Ecclesiastes 7:7* "I rebuke all spirits of madness and confusion that would attempt to oppress my mind in the name of Jesus"
- *Luke 16:9* "Let me reach and touch you so that I will be healed by your virtue"
- *Psalm 118:17* "I shall not die, but live, and declare the works of the Lord."
- *Psalm 147:3*" He heals the brokenhearted and binds up their wounds."

COMFORT

- *Psalm 86:17* "Show me a sign for good, that those who hate me may see it and be ashamed, because You, O Lord, have helped me and comforted me."
- *2 Corinthians 1:3* "Blessed be the God and Father of our Lord Jesus Christ the Father of mercies and God of all comfort."
- *Isaiah 51:12*" I, even I, am He that comforteth you: who art thou, that thou shouldest be afraid of a man that shall die, and of the son of man which shall be made as grass."
- *Isaiah 43:2* (NLT) "When you go through deep waters, I will be with you. When you go through rivers of difficulty, you will not drown. When you

walk through the fire of oppression, you will not be burned up; the flames will not consume you".

BATTLES

- *Joshua 1:5* "I will not fail you nor forsake you."
- *Psalm 23:5* "Thou preparest a table before me in the presence of mine enemies; thou anointest my head with oil; my cup runneth over."
- *Exodus 14:14* "The Lord will fight for you while you keep silent."

A PRAYER OF DELIVERANCE

Father, we humbly and boldly come before Your throne of grace, acknowledging You for who You are. You are Lord and our Father, which art in heaven. You are holy, just, righteous, and full of mercy and grace. We give You thanks. You said in all things give thanks, for this is the will of God concerning us. We thank you, we praise you, and we lift up our voices to You and bless Your holy name. Let our prayer be set before You as incense and the lifting of our hands as the evening sacrifice. Father, this day we boldly declare and decree Your Word. We stand in victory, warring a good warfare and upholding Your Word mightily before our accuser. You said that upon this rock and the acknowledgment of your kingdom, we will always triumph in Christ, and the gates of hell shall not prevail against the Kingdom of God. Oh Lord my God, You said that all who are heavy and burdened should come to You and cast our cares on You, for You care for us, and You are great and mighty.

Father, heal the brokenhearted. Father, You said whatsoever we bind on earth is bound in heaven, and what is loosed on earth is loosed in heaven. We come with the blood of Jesus against every devil that oppresses Your people. We bind the strongman of heaviness, deep-seated hurts, emotional pain, heaviness of the spirit and heart, bitterness, self-pity, sorrow, grief, despair, dejection, depression, torn spirit, rejection, unforgiveness, insomnia, suicidal thoughts, shame, hate, and hopelessness. Lord, we loose Your Word to give unto them *beauty for ashes*, the oil of joy for mourning, the garment of praise for the spirit of heaviness. We loose the love of God, the spirit of truth and life, peace, a sound mind, unity, restoration, and forgiveness. This is the confidence that we have in the Father that if we ask anything according to Your will, You hear us. By faith, we declare peace in our mind, peace, healing and joy be with our children. We strike against every hindrance in our lives that would keep us from living a fruitful life. We are confident that You hear us when we pray. We stand boldly in faith, believing that we have received as we prayed, knowing You are with us always, in Jesus' most holy, and precious name we pray. AMEN!

The Lord bless thee and keep thee. I pray the Lord cause your hands to obtain wealth and to prosper. I call you healed, I call you blessed, and I call you whole. You will live and not die. In everything, give thanks, for this is the will of God in Christ Jesus concerning you.

You will emerge UNSCARRED!

"For I will close up thy scar, and will heal thee of thy wounds, saith the Lord. Because they have called thee, O Sion, an outcast: This is she that hath none to seek after her" (Jeremiah 30:17, DRB).

REFERENCES

"Divorce Suicide Statistics." NonProfitFacts.com - Tax-Exempt Organizations. Accessed February 12, 2016. http://www.nonprofitfacts.com/MD/National-Institute-For-Healthcare-Research.html. "National Library of Medicine - National Institutes of Health." U.S. National Library of Medicine. Accessed February 12, 2016. https://www.nlm.nih.gov/.Lee, Amy. "Kids Of Divorce And Suicide: New Study Shows Link." The Huffington Post. January 24, 2011. Accessed February 12, 2016. http://www.huffingtonpost.com/2011/01/24/divorce-and-suicidal-idea_n_812456.html. "Instruments for Suicide Risk Assessment [Internet]." National Center for Biotechnology Information. Accessed February 12, 2016. https://www.ncbi.nlm.nih.gov/pubmedhealth/?term=Suicide. "Domesticviolenceroundtable.org." Domesticviolenceroundtable.org. Accessed February 12, 2016. http://www.domesticviolenceroundtable.org/.Women, New Hope for. New Hope for Women. Accessed February 12, 2016. http://www.newhopeforwomen.org/direct-services.

Kelly, Thomas M., and Dennis C. Daley. "Integrated Treatment of Substance Use and Psychiatric Disorders."

Social work in public health. 2013. Accessed February 12, 2016. https://www.ncbi.nlm.nih.gov/pmc/articles/PMC3753025/.

"Our Cheatin' Hearts." WebMD. Accessed February 12, 2016. http://www.webmd.com/men/features/our-cheating-hearts#1.

Eckhardt, John. *Prayers That Rout Demons*. Lake Mary, FL: Charisma House, 2008.

Munroe, Dr. Myles. *The Purpose and Power of Love and Marriage*. Shippensburg, PA: Destiny Image Publishers, 2002.

"1906 San Francisco earthquake." Wikipedia. March 22, 2017. Accessed February 12, 2016.https://en.wikipedia.org/wiki/1906_San_Francisco_ea rth-quake.

"The National Domestic Violence Hotline | Get Back Your ...". N.p., n.d. Web. 12 Feb. 2016 <http://www.thehotline.org/2013/07/tips-for-economic-recovery/>.

Effects of Domestic Violence on Children, http://www.domesticviolenceroundtable.org/effect-on-children.html (accessed Feb 12, 2016).

Abuser tricks and warning signs of domestic abuse. - http://www.newhopeforwomen.org/abuser-tricks (accessed Feb 12, 2016.

Cycle of Violence | Women's Center, http://web.uri.edu/womenscenter/cycle-of-violence/ (accessed Feb 12, 2016).

Why Do Smart Women Date Abusive Men? | HuffPost, http://www.huffingtonpost.com/hayley-rose-horzepa/abusive-relationships-women_b_ (accessed Feb 12, 2016).

"Values Development." Changingminds.org. http://changingminds.org/explanations_development (accessed February12, 2017).

An Empirical Inquiry to Psychological Variables http://www.jpanafrican.org/docs/vol7no3/7.3-14-Busari.pdf (accessed June 01, 2017).

Divorce and Suicide | Jason Kohlmeyer - JDSupra, http://www.jdsupra.com/legalnews/divorce-and-suicide-70107/ (accessed June 01, 2017).

"Washington Pediatric Therapy | Building A Brighter Future ...". N.p., n.d. Web. 21 Jul. 2017 <http://washingtonpediatrictherapy.com/>.

ABOUT THE AUTHOR

Angela is a proud native of Daly City, California a small suburb located on the outskirts of San Francisco. Angela is an Author, Speaker, and a Certified Coach. She's a favored mother of three, entrepreneur, and founder of ADH Enterprises, LLC. When not writing, Angela can be found serving her ministry. She is a family member of This Is Pentecost Fellowship Ministries under the tutelage of Quentin and Tamara Bennett. Angela is a twenty-four-year Federal Employee; she focuses on the social and economic wellbeing of the socially, and mentally distressed, injured veterans, widows, and orphans. As the Lord would have it, this career enables her to operate in James 1:27 on a daily basis.

At an early age, Angela wrestled with fear, rejection, low self-esteem, and insecurity. By the age of twenty, alcoholism was the driving force to her recklessness and despondency. This led to an unforgettable car crash that should have taken her life. Only by the mercy of God, she lived to tell her story. In her attempt to make life work, she found herself divorced with three children at the prime of her life. As she was *growing* through her painful divorce and childhood emotional issues, it was a prophetic word that changed the course of Angela D. Holmes' life. God had anointed her to write her story of struggle and pain so that divorced and emotionally hurting are healed and set free. God launched a course correction that catapulted her into her purpose. She chose to dedicate her life to what God had called her to do.

Angela has a relentless passion for those who struggle to heal from divorce. Her message is bold and full of faith; teaching others how to build on God's truth about who they are and learn to focus forward in spite of their past. She lives by her quote, "What we think about the most is what is driving us. What we yield to the most is what is controlling us!"

Angela focuses on encouraging, provoking, inspiring, empowering and teaching women how to maximize every moment of their life. She loves to see others shine and live free from emotional struggles, as well as learn how to take-action and move forward. She is adamant that you need someone who has been there and came out well to stand with you and walk you through the tender process of recovering from the traumatic residuals of divorce, to be your best, and create meaningful, transformative emotional growth. Being a divorced mom of three, she knows firsthand how difficult it is to shift your mindset, find emotional mastery and the desire to pick yourself up out of that corner and dust yourself off.

She is now a beacon of light, life, and hope to all who have experienced divorce and are struggling with emotional upheavals and distress. She's a Cali girl who loves chocolate, the beach, and long drives. Today, Angela resides in Northern California, fulfilling purpose with her three incredible children, Alexandra, La Nair II, and Myles.

To connect with Angela:

- Facebook: Angela D. Holmes Fan Page
- www.angeladholmes.com
- Instagram: @angeladholmes
- YouTube: Angela D. Holmes

Beauty in the Midst of Chaos

www.ingramcontent.com/pod-product-compliance
Lightning Source LLC
Chambersburg PA
CBHW070026100426
42740CB00013B/2606